ACTION

ACTION!

Reflections from the gospel of Mark.

S. Robert Maddox

ACTION

Published by Redefining Faith Resources

Scripture quotations are from The Holy Bible, English Standard Version® (ESV®), copyright © 2001 by Crossway, a publishing ministry of Good News Publishers. Used by permission. All rights reserved.

Copyright © 2013 by S. Robert Maddox

No portion of this publication may be reproduced, stored in a retrieval system or transmitted in any form by any means - except for brief quotations in published reviews - without the prior written permission of the author.

ISBN: 978-0-98900-277-6

DEDICATION

To congregations in the following communities:
Seattle, Washington
Kirkland, Washington
Livingston, Montana
Billings, Montana
Rapid City, South Dakota
Spearfish, South Dakota
Marshall, Minnesota
Mount Prospect, Illinois
Palos Heights/Orland Park, Illinois

And

To board members, administrators, faculty, staff and students of
Trinity Bible College
Ellendale, North Dakota

Thank you for enriching the lives of me and my family.

CONTENTS

Foreword	R. Steven Warner	1
Introduction	Knowing Jesus	3
Chapter 1	Good News	9
Chapter 2	Something New	17
Chapter 3	Misunderstood	25
Chapter 4	Listen and Learn	33
Chapter 5	Crisis	41
Chapter 6	Keep Walking	49
Chapter 7	Offended	57
Chapter 8	Rest	65
Chapter 9	Traditions	73
Chapter 10	Wonder-What-Wow	83
Chapter 11	Consequences	91
Chapter 12	Bartimaeus	101
Chapter 13	Authority	109

Chapter 14	Mountain-moving Prayer	119
Chapter 15	Accused	127
Chapter 16	Loose Ends	137
Chapter 17	Dying	145
Chapter 18	Denying	155
Chapter 19	The Cross	165
Chapter 20	Relationships	173
Epilogue	Perfect	183
	Acknowledgements	185
	About the Author	187
	Books by the Author	189

FOREWORD

Bob Maddox and I have been ministerial colleagues and neighboring pastors for over two decades. We've sat on numerous boards and committees together, discovering in so doing an assortment of common passions and interests.

But most importantly, what started out as a professional relationship has gradually morphed into something much more enduring and meaningful. Simply stated, Bob is my friend—a cherished friend of the first order.

One of the common interests we share is communication—speaking, listening, presenting, and writing. Bob is supremely gifted in all four genres. As many have discovered, in the arena of communication he is a quadruple threat.

Some time ago, Bob started blogging. The book

you are about to read is made up of some of his weekly blogs. This compilation is an assortment of columns that bear witness to his insights springing from his author's listening ear, speaker's voice, presenter's unique viewpoint, and writer's deft touch.

I don't need to convince you to buy this book because you already have. So, let me congratulate you on your choice of this little volume because it is chock full of wisdom. You are about to read some of the great advice that I've been blessed to hear in person over the course of many years.

This book is the next best thing to having a cup of coffee with the author. Read, be challenged, enjoy, be blessed.

Rogers Steven Warner
East Bridgewater, MA

INTRODUCTION
KNOWING JESUS

My wife and I regularly visit the Holy Land. In earlier trips, we would host a tour guided by Isaac, a very hospitable orthodox Jew. When traveling on the bus to various sights, he and I would often discuss religion. In one conversation, he bunched all Christians into one group. I tried to explain there are different kinds of Christians. He replied, "You all believe in Jesus, don't you?" I said, "Yes, but…." Before I could finish, he said, "Then you are all Christian." There was no convincing him otherwise.

An Episcopal priest writing a magazine article took a similar approach, suggesting various affiliations have collectively contributed to the final mosaic of the Church. Starting with the Liturgical church, transitioning to the Mainline church, moving to the Evangelical church and concluding with the

Pentecostal church, he wrote about each group's strengths and weaknesses.

He complimented Spirit-filled churches for their emphasis on the blessing of the Holy Spirit and for elevating the importance of the supernatural in faith. He saw their weakness as a shallow knowledge of the Lord Jesus. He considered Pentecostals anemic in understanding the Gospel writings and, with all their talk about the Savior, did not know Him very well.

The indictment caused me to examine my own reading habits. I had to admit my New Testament studies centered mainly on the writings of Paul. I was lax in regularly looking at Matthew, Mark, Luke, and John and committed myself to doing an aggressive reading of the books.

I started by examining a Harmony of the Gospels—two times successively. After looking at the book of Acts (Luke's writings being a two-volume edition), I studied each gospel narrative individually. The Episcopal priest was right; I did not know Jesus; I was telling others about someone I did not fully comprehend.

Some scholars call themselves "Red-letter Christians", referring to the statements of Jesus being printed in red by a few Bible publishers. Although not a member, I attempt to read through the entire Bible yearly, but also give the Gospels a second reading.

The first three New Testament books, known as the *synoptic* gospels, show the life of Jesus from a parallel point-of-view. As a teenager reading the Bible for the first time, I wondered why Matthew, Mark, and Luke recorded events similarly. The three writers give an accurate account of Jesus, viewing Him from different perspectives and describing Him to distinct audiences. The fourth gospel, John, is a bonus feature playing an equally important role.

Through the years, my wife and I have enjoyed looking at new homes, gleaning floor plans and decorating ideas. We occasionally will come upon a newly built house while driving and stop to peek through the windows. When viewing the same room from various windows, we see things slightly different. Similarly, by looking in all the gospel *windows*, a clearer picture about the life and times of Christ is revealed.

In my earlier years of following Jesus, the four gospels were simply history books, written to give general facts and information about the Son of God. I did not recognize the personal benefits from reading stories of events occurring centuries earlier. A college professor expanded my perspective. The Apostle John indicates not everything Jesus did was recorded. The gospels include carefully selected stories. The historical events chosen were designed to help awaken non-believers to the *need* of faith, and also *increase* the faith of believers.

I started a new habit of praying before reading and studying the gospels, asking for the stories to mold and shape my spiritual formation. While reading, I asked myself questions: Why was this particular incident recorded? What transforming benefit did this event have to the initial audience and original readers? What in these stories can help me tackle current challenges and situations?

The second gospel writer is thought to be John Mark, the one accompanying Paul and Barnabas on their first missionary journey. He may have written in Rome, describing events witnessed by the Apostle Peter, and designing the content for Romans, more than for Jews or Greeks. The readers were culturally like today, technologically advanced for their era and gleaning knowledge from various customs. He wrote a concise account of Jesus to extremely industrious people. The narrative is filled with action, another quality of contemporary life. The gospel begins abruptly and proceeds rapidly from one episode to another.

Mark, inspired by the Holy Spirit, records a stirring account of the life, suffering, death, and resurrection of Jesus. Following the Christ was becoming more difficult around the time of its writing. Some believers were being treated cruelly. Torture was on the increase and death was not out of the question. Described for believers in every generation is the *perfect model* for experiencing hardships and facing difficulties. The Anointed One shows how to handle both the ongoing and unexpected stresses of life.

If it happened to Jesus, it can happen to you—if they did it to Jesus, they may do it to you.

The chapters of *ACTION* are personal reflections based on subjects generated by reading Mark's *action* narrative of Jesus. The book became a personal ambition because of the thoughts written about death (Chapter 17). My hope is for your race of faith to benefit by reflectively reading at spiritual rest stops. Jesus is the Way, the Truth, and the Life. His story is eternally transforming!

CHAPTER ONE

GOOD NEWS

"The beginning of the gospel of Jesus Christ, the Son of God.... Now after John was arrested, Jesus came into Galilee, proclaiming the gospel of God, and saying, 'The time is fulfilled, and the kingdom of God is at hand; repent and believe in the gospel.'" (Mark 1:1, 14-15)

Mark starts his narrative by briefly revealing the ministry of John the baptizer, as prophesied by Isaiah, and states Jesus' public ministry began when John was imprisoned. He also records the first statement made by Jesus as His ministry began.

In public speaking, the introduction sets the tone for everything that follows. What foundation was Jesus building for His audience? What did He want clearly understood about the purpose of His coming?

What Jesus said and did is eternally linked to these recorded words.

"The time is fulfilled…"

When John's voice was silenced, Jesus' ministry began. The forerunner of the Anointed One, the Messiah, the Christ, had come to clear the way, to construct a straight path, and to make an understandable route. People were looking for a national leader, a deliverer from political tyranny. To comprehend God's plan, a course correction was required.

John proclaimed the problem was sin, not Rome; the problem was a corrupt heart, not a cruel nation. The deluded heart was creating corrosion, causing insincere worship, improper thinking, unwholesome behavior, and immoral activity. His mission was to break up the hard soil of the human soul, barren of truth, and make it ready for spiritual seed.

Jesus waited for the right time. As long as the forerunner was active, His ministry would not be activated. John awakened the need for everlasting freedom. People began recognizing the problem of sin, were feeling remorse over sin, and were willing to eradicate sin. The forerunner established the right setting to initiate the solution, then left the stage.

The time was also right in world circumstances.

The Greco Empire had produced a common language. The Roman Empire had established the "Pax Romana" (the peace of Rome) and built an efficient highway system. The infrastructure was suitably designed to communicate to the world His message of hope and grace.

"When the fullness of time had come, God sent forth his Son, born of woman, born under the law, to redeem those who were under the law, so that we might receive adoption as sons. And because you are sons, God has sent the Spirit of his Son into our hearts, crying, 'Abba! Father!' So you are no longer a slave, but a son, and if a son, then an heir through God. (Galatians 4:4-7)

Jesus said, "It's time!"

"The kingdom of God is at hand..."

The divine kingdom is no longer distant and unattainable, but within reach. The kingdom came in the person of Jesus—someone seen, heard, and touched. John the baptizer prepared the way, and Jesus is "the Way, the Truth, and the Life." (John 14:6) Jews believed in two totally separate ages: the present sinful age, and the future age when evil is destroyed. In Jesus, the *future* invaded the *present*.

The Kingdom of God is progressively revealed: *The kingdom was first revealed in ancient Israel,*

God demonstrating His plan through a specific people.

The kingdom was further revealed in Jesus, giving clarity to the Covenant.

The kingdom is presently revealed in the Church, believers powerfully and supernaturally affirming His presence.

The kingdom will be revealed in the Millennial Reign—a thousand years of holy rest and divine peace, giving testimony of a world without the evil one.

The kingdom will be fully experienced in a new heaven and new earth—a universe centered on New Jerusalem and inhabited with God's people.

By following Jesus, the kingdom is present and will be experienced abundantly when evil is banished.

What is the kingdom of God? The Kingdom is divine *power in action*, God claiming His right over the satan and the sinful course of this world. By expressing Himself in all of the creation and asserting His divine authority over the evil empire, an alarm sounds that causes the corrupt world to enter into crisis and chaos.

The kingdom is righteousness, peace, and joy in

the Holy Spirit (Romans 14:17), essential attributes giving evidence of His reign. His power gives believers the *capability* to live pure and moral lives, the *ability* to effectively tell His story to others, and the *means* to manifest supernatural signs and wonders.

Followers of Jesus are to unceasingly seek every dimension of His kingdom, desiring the full impact of His presence. With earnest and sincere faith, they can resist sin, selfishness, and the satan. The Kingdom is not experienced if faith becomes compromised—seldom praying, neglecting Scripture, and rarely gathering together. The kingdom is near, and believers are to act accordingly.

"Repent and…"

The way to God's kingdom involves *an about face*, turning around. Radical change is involved in Kingdom living. The word "repent" means *a change of mind*.

Repentance means someone once loving sin now hates it, taking responsibility for unacceptable conduct and seeking new behavior, ending wrongful practices and living in right ways. Repenting does not include punishing oneself for past mistakes, hating oneself for past failures, and depressing oneself with a sense of worthlessness. The past is over—learn from it but avoid being ruled by it.

Throw out corrupt thoughts, actions, and memories by entering into divinely given transformation.

There is a difference between sorrow for consequences and hating sin. Some feel bad about the mess sin has brought upon them but would keep sinning if they could be reasonably sure of escaping the consequences. They do not hate sin but despise consequences and dislike getting caught.

A Sunday School teacher asked the class what repentance meant? A little boy said, "It is being sorry for your sins." A little girl said, "It is being sorry enough to quit."

"Believe in the gospel."

His proclamation ends with a word about belief, *taking Jesus at His word*. Believe God loves the world so much that He provided a priceless and precious sacrifice to free His creation. Believe God is as just and gracious as Jesus reveals Him to be. Believe what sounds too good to be true is genuine.

The pronouncement made by Jesus at the onset of His ministry is the foundation of everything He said and did and is the bedrock for following Him today.

ACTION

The time to start experiencing God's kingdom is

now. Will you follow Jesus and come under His leadership? Are you receptive to a total turnaround?

You cannot live a *perfect* life, but you can live a *forgiven* life. Instead of wandering aimlessly away from God, turn and head toward Him. Ask Jesus to reign over every moment of your day. In Biblical terms, realize you have sinned and come short of the glory of God, repent of your sin, and make Jesus your Lord. The conversation with the Heavenly Father does not have to be long, but sincere.

PRAYER

"Heavenly Father, thank you for making a way for me to enter Your kingdom. I realize there will never be enough goodness in me to earn access. Please forgive me for my rebellion and waywardness.

"Lord Jesus, reign completely over my life and fill me with Your presence. I ask for the Holy Spirit to help me abide in You and live for You. Thank you for what You have done and am about to do. Amen!"

CHAPTER TWO

SOMETHING NEW

No one sews a piece of unshrunk cloth on an old garment. If he does, the patch tears away from it, the new from the old, and a worse tear is made. And no one puts new wine into old wineskins. If he does, the wine will burst the skins—and the wine is destroyed, and so are the skins. But new wine is for fresh wineskins." (Mark 2:21-22)

If you were asked to draw a picture of God, how would you sketch Him? What features would you give? Would He be a man in his thirties, with the facial appearance and skin tone of someone from the Middle East? Would you avoid giving a distinct form and place a hazy figure on a majestic throne with beams of light? Would you attempt to show divinity as a kind of energy force or a modern-day action hero?

Children often describe God as someone very old. Even adults have a perception of a weary and worn grandfather type. He is not old; He is timeless. He is new every day! He is only as old as you make Him; His ways are only as monotonous as you determine; His activities are only as predictable as you imagine. The entire Bible reveals the newness of God.

God did something new

Children begin when conceived in the mother's womb. People establish themselves with a beginning date—a birthday. The Lord has always existed and sees the past, present, and future altogether.

At a point in eternity, God took counsel with Himself and decided to do *something new*. He created the universe. The One who always was, always is, and always will be, started the cosmos out of nothing. The materials of creation were *all new*. Upon the earth, He commands creatures to live, creatures of infinite variety able to live in a life-sustaining environment. He caps off the act of creation by personally forming a man in His own image and likeness. All things were *new*. Nothing like this had ever happened before.

God made people with the ability to reason, consider choices, and render decisions. The first human rebelled, he sinned. The relationship with

ACTION

God was severed, yet He purposed in His heart to limit the time and set out to provide a *new way* to connect.

Through centuries filled with good and bad, God eventually considered a person named Abraham as a "friend of God"—a *new kind of relationship*. God pronounced to Abraham, "Through your seed the nations of the world will be blessed." (Genesis 22:18) He would be used to restore what was lost by sin.

Abraham had a son Isaac, who had a son Jacob, who had twelve sons. To develop the family into a tribe, and eventually into a nation, God brought them into the protective surroundings of Egypt. After four hundred years, the family became a *nation within a nation*, and Pharaoh's security turned to tyranny.

God raised up a deliverer named Moses and revealed Himself through the written Law—*something new*. The Law was profitable for describing the magnitude of sin, but most failed to grasp the message and mistakenly believed established rules could be perfectly obeyed. The Law was designed to expose the impossibility of living a faultless life, demonstrating the need of a Savior and Deliverer from sin.

Everyone is condemned and unable to meritoriously save themselves. Goodness has never been a ticket to heaven. Only grace through faith restores a relationship with God. Goodness is meant to flow out of a *new* love relationship.

When I regularly wore suits, friends would sometimes comment about an eye-catching tie or a nice-looking shirt. The compliment belonged to my wife. I was not a sharp dresser before getting married. We got married and, out of love, she showed me how to select suits and accessories complimenting my appearance. Similarly, out of a love relationship with God, people can become better.

After the Law was written, God brought Israel to a special land and did *something new*—He led them to victory. Israel did not *acquire* the land but was given the land, and the Lord became their King. No other nation had such a distinction. This was *new* and unique.

As the nation became established, years filled with joy and hardship, wars and victories, kings and captivities, God *continued doing new things*. He revealed Himself constantly in *new ways*. He faithfully made Himself known to a stubborn people. Many today are equally inflexible, and He does not give up on them either. He continually reaches out to people possessing unbending hearts.

In the fullness of time, the Son of God

appeared—*something new*. Jesus came and walked among people; the Creator became one of the created. He fulfilled the Law and brought forth the church, *a new community*, the embodiment of His presence.

God did not put the *new message* of grace into the old structure of Law. The Good News is *totally different*, disrupting old ways and bursting ancient molds. Jesus fulfills the earlier message and places a new hope into a new structure, involving *new birth* and *new life*.

No longer are there tablets of stone, but testimonies of salvation. The new formation includes the Lord taking residency in people of faith. The relationship changes from *God with us* to *God in us*, believers being the *new temple* in which He dwells. The Spirit moving over the face of the earth now abides in the hearts of His followers, providing strength and victory.

From the beginning until now God *has been doing new things*.

God is still doing something new

God has not stopped doing *new*; have you quit looking? "Behold, I am doing a new thing; now it springs forth, do you not perceive it? I will make a way in the wilderness and rivers in the desert."

(Isaiah 43:19)

God always has *new ways* for His people. He comes upon a dry and thirsty heart and brings a new river of life. He renews broken lives, makes stale homes fresh, and invigorates depleted churches. God is very much in the business of *making all things new*.

If you let Him, God can do something new in your life. If presently not a follower of Jesus, He can give you a *new destiny*. If in a relationship with God, He can give you a *new outlook*—unspoiled desires, energies, and ambitions. If you have been following Jesus for a long time, He can bring *new vitality* to every part of your life. He longs to give you a fresh touch of His Spirit.

There comes a time when patching is insufficient and creating new must occur. Sometimes things become patched when total abandonment of the old and acceptance of the new is necessary. Wineskins, when new, have a certain amount of elasticity. As they grow old, they become hard and unyielding. Jesus wants pliability in His followers.

I once read a slogan, "When you reach a conclusion, you're dead." When your mind becomes fixed and settled, when you become unwilling to consider, contemplate, and accept new ways, you may be physically alive but mentally and emotionally dead. Becoming set in stale habits is fatal.

As people grow older, a constitutional dislike develops for *new and improved*, preferring *old and familiar*. Believers can grow unwilling to adjust and adapt. New heights of living require retaining an adventurous mind.

God is going to do something new

In the avenues of time, *God with us* is no longer and *God in us* will soon end—*us with God* comes next. Followers of Jesus are going to a place presently being prepared for them, where God eternally dwells. The place is called *New Jerusalem*, located in the *new heaven* and *new earth*—a place without tempter, without sin, without sorrow, without tears, and without death.

ACTION

Are you in a rut? Have things become predictable and mundane? Has deadness crept in unaware? The timeless God is continually doing new things. His ways are new and refreshing. There is no predictability in faith.

Whenever new things occur, cynicism and criticism can easily develop. Rigidity is lethal. Be open to fresh encounters with God. He longs to usher you into *new life*, and to living daily in the Spirit.

CHAPTER THREE

MISUNDERSTOOD

When his family heard it, they went out to seize him, for they were saying, "He is out of his mind." And the scribes who came down from Jerusalem were saying, "He is possessed by Beelzebul," and "by the prince of demons he casts out the demons." And he called them to him and said to them in parables, "How can Satan cast out Satan?" (Mark 3:21-23)

Mark records the thoughts, feelings, and actions of Jesus, and how people misread and actively opposed Him. His opposition came primarily from within the religious community, the very people supposedly in tune with God.

Jesus was often misunderstood—family members thought him crazy and critics considered him demon-possessed. As a follower of Jesus, divine opportunities can lead to disapproval by people who know better, even defamation of character. Are those closest to you thinking you have lost your mind and those critical of you questioning the source of your actions?

"You have lost your mind!"

Matthew records a troubling comment of Jesus: "Do not think that I have come to bring peace to the earth. I have not come to bring peace, but a sword. For I have come to set a man against his father, and a daughter against her mother, and a daughter-in-law against her mother-in-law. And a person's enemies will be those of his own household." (Matthew 10:34-36)

While in the Air Force, stationed in South Dakota, a season of spiritual refreshing occurred among the youth of a local church. A great passion rose to tell others about Jesus. Many became His followers and lives were radically transformed.

A teenager went from living a highly self-centered life to passionately developing a faith in God—reading the Bible daily, praying fervently, telling friends about Jesus, and regularly attending church. Her parents were not pleased with the changes nor appreciated her devotion to spiritual truths.

ACTION

One evening, she came to church in tears. Her mother had just forbidden her from coming any longer and said to her, "I would rather you be on drugs than attend that church." Following Jesus can unfortunately generate disapproval by those you love. The Good News can divide and impact the home.

Why did family members think Jesus was out of His mind? First, He left the family business to become an itinerant teacher, giving up home and security. Secondly, He put Himself in a head-on collision with influential people, suspending safety and entering harm's way. Thirdly, He picked the wrong kind of people to be world-changers— ambitious and levelheaded leaders do not select plain and ordinary folks. Jesus must have lost His senses.

Was his family being swayed by public opinion? His actions were getting mixed reviews. Were reports of public unrest more persuasive than testimonies of transformed lives? Were his kin attempting to bring him home for safety, or were they embarrassed? Were they ashamed and troubled about the family's reputation and public image?

Truth is never found in rumors and hearsay. Knowing Jesus as the *Son of God* is not possible without firsthand experience. "Taste and see that the Lord is good." (Psalms 34:8)

My wife and I wanted our nieces to know their cousins better and, one summer, invited them to spend a few weeks in our home. My brother refused! A niece eventually told us that he thought I had joined a cult. A price for following Jesus may include family members thinking you are crazy.

If people closest to you reject your decision to follow Jesus, do not reject them. Stay connected! Mary's other children eventually recognized Jesus as the Son of God and your family may someday recognize your relationship with Him.

"Where are you coming from?"

Why people become critical of others is difficult to pinpoint. Scorn can come from disliking appearance or misreading actions.

Some have unreasonable and unreachable standards. If you do not sound or appear holy, you are *carnal*. Failing to use pious terminology offends religious people.

Others may not like your actions. Your behavior does not meet an excessive *criterion* of virtue. Failing to live by burdensome demands upsets religious people. Critics easily find fault instead of affirming the truth.

Jesus' critics speculated He was associated with

the demon god, Beelzebub ("lord of the flies"), or Beelzebul ("the dung-god"). Exorcised demons were confessing and acknowledging His Lordship. Was this causing confusion? The outburst of demons being cast out may have baffled people about the source of His actions. Critics, with envy and spiritual bigotry, embellished the truth or fabricated a lie.

How do you deal with criticism? Before you tune them out, ask yourself if it is true? Your critics may be right.

E. Stanley Jones, one-time missionary to India, wrote, "May I add a word of personal testimony? No one in public work can escape criticism. I have had my share. It used to cut me to the quick. But now when criticism comes I find myself asking, 'Is it true?' If so, I will take it, will profit from it. My critics thus become 'the unpaid watchmen of my soul.' If the criticism is not true, I can still use it. I can make these fires of unjust criticism serve to burn up my fetters and make me free." (The Christ of Every Road, pp. 239-240)

When providing leadership to a college, I had many advisors. Blending together the request of board members, administrators, faculty, staff, students, alumni, pastors, church leaders, government agencies, and accrediting associations was taxing. I tried to comply with every request.

Occasionally, desires and wishes were in direct conflict with one another. Someone was going to be disappointed.

Two questions became the ruling force of my actions: What is the right thing to do, and are my actions being done with a right attitude? If not careful, criticism can steer you down a wrong path and move you further away from God's plan. Never allow criticism to rule your actions. Influence? Maybe! Rule? No!

Keep trying to communicate to critics. Jesus tried to talk to them, without defending Himself. Adversaries usually do not accept explanations; they have already made up their mind. No number of words will ever justify your actions.

God is your sole Vindicator; no one defends you better. Hopefully, your opponents will reconsider and come to a different conclusion. Until then, do right acts with a right heart, and He will help you handle the sting of criticism. He hurts with you in every injustice.

Maybe you should look at criticism differently? J.G. Morrison tells a story about John Wesley, founder of the Methodist church. One day, while riding along on a road, he realized three days had passed without suffering persecution—no brick or egg had been thrown at him. Alarmed, he stopped his horse and exclaimed, "Can it be that I have sinned and am backslidden?" Getting off his steed, Wesley went down on his knees and began audibly interceding with God to show where, if any, there had been a fault.

A man, on the other side of a hedge, heard the praying, looked and recognized the preacher. Not liking Wesley, he picked up a brick and tossed it toward him. The stone missed, harmlessly falling beside him. Wesley leaped to his feet joyfully and said, "Thank God, it's all right; I still have His presence."

Is your testimony worth a thrown brick?

ACTION

Swearing loses its intended purpose if done regularly and should be generally avoided. Cuss words, however, perform a function in human language. Besides providing an instant release of pent-up frustration, restoring emotional equilibrium quicker, they send a signal for others to pay closer attention.

Read carefully: Sometimes in life, you go through feelings like you are "damned if you do, *and* damned if you don't." Frustrating! When between a rock and hard place, do what is *right*, which often runs opposite of *popular*.

Those closest to you may think you are crazy, and those critical of you may question your actions. If family, friend, or foe rejects you, love them. Gain your peace in God and let Him deal with them.

If it happened to Jesus it can happen to you—if they did it to Jesus they may do it to you.

CHAPTER FOUR

LISTEN AND LEARN

Again, he began to teach beside the sea. And a very large crowd gathered about him, so that he got into a boat and sat in it on the sea, and the whole crowd was beside the sea on the land. And he was teaching them many things in parables ... And when he was alone, those around him with the twelve asked him about the parables. And he said to them, "To you has been given the secret of the kingdom of God, but for those outside everything is in parables, so that "they may indeed see but not perceive, and may indeed hear but not understand, lest they should turn and be forgiven." And he said to them, "Do you not understand this parable? How then will you understand all the parables? ... And he said to them, "Is a lamp brought in to be put under a basket, or under a bed, and not on a stand? For nothing is hidden except to be made manifest; nor is anything secret except to come to light. If anyone has ears to hear, let him hear." ... With many such parables he spoke the word to them, as they were able to hear it. He did not speak to them without a parable, but privately to his own disciples he explained everything. (Mark 4: 1-2, 10-13, 21-23, 33-34)

Teaching professionals understand helping someone learn demands variety. Everyone approaches and understands study material differently. Creating mental images with words is critical for making a lesson clear. Storytelling paints pictures in the mind, and Jesus was a masterful storyteller.

Parables are everyday life situations that teach moral and spiritual truths. They are often simple but significant in learning about God. Jesus used them to describe Kingdom mysteries, such as, what is it, how is it manifested, who belongs in it, and what lifestyle reflects it?

Among the crowd listening to Jesus was a group known as *the Twelve*—hand-selected men on an extraordinary journey. He had special plans for them and was investing personal time into their training. They often wondered, "What is He saying; why doesn't He speak plainly?"

My childhood home overlooked the fishermen's

wharf in Seattle. A friend's dad owned a fleet of fishing boats that trolled the Alaskan waters every summer. We occasionally went to the docks to look at the various watercrafts and watch the crews preparing for departure. The sailors I met spoke plainly and directly.

The group specially selected by Jesus, mostly ordinary fishermen, was often confused by His lessons. The One not wanting any to perish taught in ways leaving crowds wondering.

No one likes to appear dumb but some of the parables were hard to understand. The Twelve came to Jesus privately and asked, "What is the meaning of these stories?" He responded with a question, "Don't you have ears that hear?" In other words, are you simply hearing with your mind or *listening with your heart*?

A more extended account of the dialogue between Jesus and the Twelve is recorded in Matthew: "Indeed, in their case, the prophecy of Isaiah is fulfilled that says: 'You will indeed hear but never understand, and you will indeed see but never perceive.' For this people's heart has grown dull, and with their ears they can barely hear, and their eyes they have closed, lest they should see with their eyes and hear with their ears and understand with their heart and turn, and I would heal them." (Matthew

13:14-15)

The gospel writer quoted from Isaiah 6, describing the prophet coming face to face with his uncleanness and the Lord touching his lips with purifying fire. Without divine cleansing, Kingdom living is difficult to understand. Out of purity comes a greater awareness of His presence. Ears and eyes, once dull and blind, can better comprehend eternal truths.

Some today hopelessly wonder about the meaning of life, their judgments dulled by carelessness. Greed, pride, and envy numb the mind, making it unable to comprehend God's ways. How can you grasp divine truths?

Be a disciple

"When he was alone with his own *disciples*, he explained everything." (v. 34) A major difference between *conversion* and *discipleship* is that conversion requires a *decision* and discipleship requires a *journey*. Some decide to join but fail to enter the journey.

Four distinctions reveal those traveling with Jesus:

First, *disciples give evidence of being with Him.* The crowd knew those who walked with Him. They were always together, spending time with Him. It is equally evident today when someone is on a journey with Jesus.

Before placing faith in God, I was part of a rock band, popular with high school students, and regularly partied. After deciding to follow Jesus, more time was invested in Him. I grew increasingly uncomfortable doing former activities. Friends who knew me for years were seeing definite changes. Is there evidence you are with Jesus?

Secondly, *disciples are followers.* Followers are not in front, nor stand beside, but stay behind. No one is greater or equal to the Lord. Followers identify with John the baptizer, who said, "He must become greater; I must become less." (John 3:30)

I heard someone once say, "I want to be right beside Jesus when He returns so I can give Satan the first blow." Jesus longs to fight your battles for you. The appropriate position is *behind* Him.

Thirdly, *disciples are students.* Students study! They are aware they know little about God and apply themselves to learn more in the classroom of life.

College studies taught me two things: how much I do not know, and the need of endurance to finish well. Never quit seeking greater clarity about the designs and purposes of God.

Finally, *disciples are teachable.* Prerequisites for teaching are not position, possessions, or prestige. Everything and everyone can teach you.

A church I attended while in college had a weekly nursing home service where I would occasionally help. A mentally-challenged church member passionately participated in all the services. He may have had analytical limitations, but I watched him dealing with residence; his actions gave a lesson about loving the unlovely unconditionally.

Understanding the ways of God requires being a disciple.

Possess an "asking" nature

The Twelve *asked* Him about the parables. (v. 10) "If any of you lacks wisdom, let him ask God, who gives generously to all without reproach, and it will be given him." (James 1:5) "You do not have, because you do not ask." (James 4:2)

Asking stems from a deep-seated love for God, and a desire for His plan to be accomplished. Discipleship involves asking for insight, with the goal of devotedly doing His will. "Ask and it will be given to you…." (Luke 11:9) Luke grammatically indicates the asking is *continual*. You are to possess an asking *nature*.

I regularly hosted special speakers at church. A guest one year clearly and concisely communicated life-changing truths from the Bible. Feeling unable to do the same, I asked him to examine my library and recommend additional books. Glancing briefly at my collection, he said, "You have everything you need!" and went on to say, "Most ministers fail to prepare their heart. Study Scripture prayerfully, with your heart open to the voice of the Spirit, and He will guide you into all truth."

Jesus desires to illumine the soul of His followers. It starts by asking.

Listen and do

"Consider carefully what you hear. With the measure you *use*, it will be measured to you—and even more." (v. 24) Willingness to act is necessary before the truth is revealed. Are you willing to do whatever He commands?

Included in my college studies were two years of Greek, giving me the ability to sing, speak, and read the language. After the academic regiment ended, my usage changed. Today, I can still comfortably use a Greek Lexicon and pronounce words correctly but have lost many skills *by the lack of use*.

What happens in language skills can happen in

spiritual formation. Failing to act leads to decline. The mysteries of grace and mercy are not for the lazy and indifferent. Retaining truth requires action.

ACTION

Are you as close to the Lord as you once were? Do you still know His voice and comprehend His counsel?

Pastors regularly hear people say, "I just don't sense His presence like I use to!" or, "I don't gain direction anymore through Scripture reading and prayer." A longstanding quote reads, "If you are not as close to the Lord as you once were, guess who moved?"

Are you teachable? Are you asking and seeking truth? If He tells you His ways, will you do what He says?

Follow Jesus, stay teachable, continually ask, then listen and do.

CHAPTER FIVE

CRISIS

On that day, when evening had come, he said to them, "Let us go across to the other side." And leaving the crowd, they took him with them in the boat, just as he was. And other boats were with him. And a great windstorm arose, and the waves were breaking into the boat, so that the boat was already filling. But he was in the stern, asleep on the cushion. And they woke him and said to him, "Teacher, do you not care that we are perishing?" And he awoke and rebuked the wind and said to the sea, "Peace! Be still!" And the wind ceased, and there was a great calm. He said to them, "Why are you so afraid? Have you still no faith?" And they were filled with great fear and said to one another, "Who then is this, that even the wind and the sea obey him?" (Mark 4:35-41)

This event is familiar to anyone reading the Bible; three gospel writers record the incident. Mark, however, is more biting in his usage of words.

The mood of the moment is expressed by the boat passengers frantically shouting, "Teacher, don't you even care that we are all about to drown?" Jesus was reprimanded by friends more afraid of a storm then the One who the winds and sea obey.

Why did they even wake Jesus? Did they think He should witness their imminent demise? Was He supposed to be anxious with them? They never imagined He could stop the crisis.

His life is the story of divine intervention—sometimes delivering His followers from danger, and other times getting them through adversity. Either way, He produces calmness out of turbulence.

The word "crisis" means *to separate*—a division point. Dictionaries define it as *a decisive or crucial time; a situation whose outcome decides whether bad consequences will follow*. Everyone experiences calamity. What characteristics often surface in catastrophes?

Perplexity

The furious storm came *suddenly* and was more than a single gust of wind. The Sea of Galilee is known for abrupt storms, coming with a shattering and terrifying quickness. Anything unexpected leaves people feeling confused and wondering, "What is going on?"

No matter how well you plan and prepare, unexpected moments cannot be prevented, and perplexity follows. Should they happen, do you question God by wondering, "Lord, where are You? Don't You care?"

He cares very much! "Cast all your anxieties on him, because he cares for you." (1 Peter 5:7) "The Lord is good, a stronghold in the day of trouble; he knows those who take refuge in him." (Nahum 1:7)

When the unexpected occurs, take shelter in Jesus until He stills the storm.

Panic

The boat was at the point of being swamped and the disciples were at whit's end. Problems often lead people to panic.

Our house in a northwest suburb of Chicago had a ceiling needing replacement. The room, originally designed as a sunroom, had sixteen large, insulated glass units overhead. The seal separating the air space between the glass sections failed, causing condensation to develop. The most cost-effective way to correct the problem was to construct a different kind of roof.

A brief rain shower came shortly after the glass units were removed. Tarps minimized damage and work continued. We ran short of lumber near the top of the roof. The lumberyard was out of stock but was expecting a shipment in a day or so. We placed plastic over the exposed area and hoped the rain would hold off until the job was done.

All went well as we waited. The lumber arrived, and plans were made to complete the project the next morning, yet rain came during the night. At 10:30 PM, the plastic burst and water came pouring into the family room. I immediately went to the roof and re-installed the cover. Water quickly filled low-lying areas, requiring clearing every few minutes. The rain lasted all night, over five inches fell.

I experienced every kind of human emotion while standing on the roof throughout the night: fear, panic, anger, resentment, desperation. I prayed every type of prayer: request, rebuke, demand, ask, plead, beg, petition, thanksgiving. Quiet assurance came by accepting the problem required *going through* instead of *deliverance*. Jesus gave inward calmness throughout the time of outward crisis.

What do you do when not knowing what to do? For the disciples it meant bail water, wake up Jesus, and become free of the storm. In my situation it involved draining water, trusting Jesus, and riding out the storm. Either way, you win!

Worry

The worried boat passengers failed to grasp the full impact of following Jesus.

Worry is like a thin stream of fear trickling through the mind, cutting a channel into which all other thoughts are drained. Worry negatively affects behavior, actions, and health, lessening the quality and shortening the longevity of life.

Believers are given clear instructions on what to do during unknowing times. "Therefore, do not be anxious about tomorrow, for tomorrow will be anxious for itself. Sufficient for the day is its own trouble." (Matthew 6:34)

A Navy chaplain drew up a "Worry Table," based on problems brought to him by sailors. Their worries fit into five categories: 40% were about things that never happened; 30% were about decisions already made and not changeable; 12% were about sickness that never came; 10% were about children and friends not wanting help; 8% were about real problems. He concluded: 92% of worries are needless.

"Do not be anxious about anything, but in everything by prayer and supplication with thanksgiving let your requests be made known to God. And the peace of God, which surpasses all understanding, will guard your hearts and your minds in Christ Jesus. (Philippians 4:6-7)

A fable is told of Death walking toward a city. A man stopped Death and asked, "What are you going to do?" Death replied, "I'm going to kill 10,000 people." "That's horrible!" said the man. "That's the way it is," Death said, "that's what I do." The day passed, and the man met Death coming back, and said, "You told me you were going to kill 10,000 but I heard 70,000 died." Death said, "I only killed 10,000, worry killed the rest."

What is the remedy for worries? In the pioneer days of aviation, a pilot was making an around-the-world flight. Two hours after departing a landing field he heard a noise in the plane, the gnawing of a rat. The rodent had gotten in while his plane was refueling and, for all he knew, was gnawing a cable or critical control. Being hours away from the next landing and wondering what to do, he remembered rats cannot live at high altitudes. He climbed the plane several thousand feet and the gnawing ceased.

Worries are a rodent that cannot live in the secret place of the Most High, they cannot breathe in a heavenly atmosphere. Worries die when you ascend into His presence by reading Scripture, praying, and relying on the power of the Holy Spirit.

ACTION

A woman was facing knee surgery. She was a bit nervous and asked her boss, a veterinarian, for advice. Without hesitation he told her, "Turn your fears into prayer, rest, and don't lick your incision."

Good advice! Pray, rest in the Lord, and do not lick your wounds. They will heal.

No predicament can match Jesus. He changes crisis to calmness. When confused, not knowing what to do, and facing an unknown future, He is close by and can make things peaceful and still.

Call on Him and do what is necessary until the storm ends!

CHAPTER SIX

KEEP WALKING

And when Jesus had crossed again in the boat to the other side, a great crowd gathered about him, and he was beside the sea. Then came one of the rulers of the synagogue, Jairus by name, and seeing him, he fell at his feet and implored him earnestly, saying, "My little daughter is at the point of death. Come and lay your hands on her, so that she may be made well and live." And he went with him. And a great crowd followed him and thronged about him ... While he was still speaking, there came from the ruler's house some who said, "Your daughter is dead. Why trouble the Teacher any further?" But overhearing what they said, Jesus said to the ruler of the synagogue, "Do not fear, only believe." And he allowed no one to follow him except Peter and James and John the brother of James. They came to the house of the ruler of the synagogue, and Jesus saw a commotion, people weeping and wailing loudly. And when he had entered, he said to them, "Why are you making a commotion and weeping? The child is not dead but sleeping." And they laughed at him. But he put them all outside and took the child's father and mother and those who were with him and went in where the child was. Taking her by the hand he said to her, "Talitha cumi," which means, "Little girl, I say to you, arise." And immediately the girl got up and began walking (for she was twelve years of age), and they were immediately overcome with amazement. And he strictly charged them that no one should know this, and told them to give her something to eat. (Mark 5:21-24, 35-43)

Jairus was a respected member of the community: overseeing worship services, managing synagogue programs, allocating duties, and ensuring everything was carried out in good fashion. He goes to Jesus, asking Him to come to his house and give attention to a sick daughter. A desperate woman was healed while they journeyed to his home. The daughter died before they arrived, and Jesus raised her from the dead.

Jewish girls become women at "twelve years and one day." A 12-year-old, on the threshold of womanhood, becomes critically ill and dies. At the same time, a woman hemorrhaging for 12 years pushes through the crowd, touches Jesus, and receives healing. Ironically, death comes to a 12-year-old and a 12-year condition is healed. The year the girl was born is the same year the woman becomes ill. Did both happen the same day? Was this coincidence or providence?

The story involves *traveling*. What is required to start walking with Jesus? What happens while walking? What will be experienced if you keep walking?

Start walking

Many religious practices had been elevated and made equal with the Law. Jairus normally associated with people who saw Jesus as a threat to Jewish customs and traditions. They were uncomfortable with Him having open access to crowds and wanted His ministry stopped. Anyone enjoying the perks of privilege would naturally avoid such a controversial character, yet when the life of someone loved is threatened, caution gets thrown to the wind and restraints become discarded; a solution is more important.

What did Jairus relinquish to walk with Jesus? *He put aside prejudice.* Jesus was unorthodox to an orthodox Jew. Prejudice means to judge beforehand—a refusal to examine evidence and immediately rendering a verdict. Jairus abandoned his pre-conceived assumptions about Him.

He put aside dignity. The Ruler of the Synagogue threw himself at the feet of Jesus. Like Jairus, centuries earlier a foreign dignitary named Naaman came to the prophet Elisha for a healing. The prophet personally chose not to talk to him. His servant told the man to dip in the Jordan River seven times. Syrian Prime Ministers were not treated with such disrespect. Naaman concluded, "Aren't there far better rivers in Syria than the muddy Jordan?" But he put aside his dignity and lost his leprosy. People wanting to experience God must place smugness at the foot of Calvary's cross.

He put aside pride. In-charge leaders are uncomfortable being indebted to others. Asking Jesus for help was humbling.

When I began ministering in Chicago, I quickly attempted to get acquainted with church families. The husband of an active member did not regularly attend. The man and I made plans to have lunch together. I met an extremely nice, generous, thoughtful, and highly successful gentleman. When the bill arrived, I casually picked it up. An awkward look came to his face. I later found out he always picked up the tab at restaurants.

While leaving he said, "I owe you," and for several months would not let it rest until he found a

ACTION

way to pay me back. He was uncomfortable not having control. The very first step in gaining abundant life is realizing your indebtedness to God.

He put aside friends. Instead of sending a messenger, Jairus personally went to Jesus. How unusual for someone to leave the side of a dying child, unless no one else was willing to go.

There is strong probability many close acquaintances objected to Jesus' involvement and refused to get Him. The father defied family and friends, personally asking Jesus to come. People may think you foolish when you are clearly acting wisely.

The synagogue ruler put aside everything to walk with Jesus. The requirement is still necessary.

While walking

"While Jesus was still speaking, some men came from the house of Jairus, the synagogue ruler. 'Your daughter is dead,' they said. 'Why bother the teacher anymore?'" (V. 35) Friends attempted to stop him from walking with Jesus any further.

What was racing through the synagogue ruler's mind? He comes to Jesus, humbles himself, and associates with Him. Going to his house, they are delayed by a woman needing a miracle. Her healing may have encouraged him to believe, "Jesus healed her and will heal my daughter, too." Suddenly, he hears, "Your daughter is dead!"

He found himself on an emotional roller-coaster, built up by a miracle and torn down by devastating news—a 12-year condition healed and a 12-year-old's life ends. Did he wonder, "What if we had not been delayed and got here sooner?" Just because you are walking with Jesus does not mean every situation will go as planned; not every outcome will be pleasant.

Attempts are often made to discourage people from identifying with Jesus. You can expect intimidating comments during your faith journey. They mostly come from people you know.

Keep walking

When others try to discourage you, keep walking. Persistence is a vital part of faith. Ignore the voice of scoffers. Jesus is saying, "Just believe!"

Followers of Jesus sometimes give up too quickly and fail to experience many blessings. A church leader once said, "The thing about Christians is: When they lose, they quit! When they win, they quit! They just quit!" The power that raises people from the dead is available to those who keep walking; only then will you experience all He can do.

Dolly Parton came from a poor Appalachian family and was asked why she became successful when many other poor mountain people did not. She replied, "I never stopped trying and never tried stopping."

A plaque on a wall at a novelty store read, "If everything is coming your way, you're in the wrong lane. And when everything seems to be going against you, remember that the airplane takes off against the wind, not with it."

Do not be surprised by discouraging remarks. As you travel toward your heavenly home, attempts will be made to stop you. If you persevere, Jesus will bring you to a greater life and a deeper joy.

ACTION

Walk with Jesus, believe in Him, and enter resurrection power. Embrace this final thought:

"You Mustn't Quit," by Edgar A. Guest

When things go wrong, as they sometimes will,
When the road you're trudging seems all uphill,
When the funds are low and the debts are high,
And you want to smile but you have to sigh,
When care is pressing you down a bit,
Rest if you must but,
Don't You Quit!

Life is strange with its twists and turns,
As every one of us sometimes learns,
And many a fellow turns about,
When he might have won had he stuck it out,
Don't give up though the pace seems slow,
You may succeed with another blow.

Often the goal is nearer than,
It seems to a faint and faltering man,
Often the struggler has given up,
When he might have captured the victor's cup,
And he learned too late when the night came down,
How close he was to the golden crown.

Success is failure turned inside out,
The silver tint of the clouds of doubt,
And you never can tell how close you are,
It may be near when it seems afar,
So, stick to the fight when you're hardest hit,
It's when things seem the worst,
That You Mustn't Quit.

CHAPTER SEVEN

OFFENDED

He went away from there and came to his hometown, and his disciples followed him. And on the Sabbath he began to teach in the synagogue, and many who heard him were astonished, saying, "Where did this man get these things? What is the wisdom given to him? How are such mighty works done by his hands? Is not this the carpenter, the son of Mary and brother of James and Joses and Judas and Simon? And are not his sisters here with us?" And they took offense at him. And Jesus said to them, "A prophet is not without honor, except in his hometown and among his relatives and in his own household." And he could do no mighty work there, except that he laid his hands on a few sick people and healed them. And he marveled because of their unbelief. And he went about among the villages teaching. (Mark 6:1-6)

In the last years of my mother's life, she lived with the effects of a debilitating stroke. She worked hard to recover some mobility but never regained the means to communicate clearly. Her mind was sharp, but she was unable to make short phrases or complete sentences. She conversed on the phone with single word responses. As far as I knew, her life was going well, but she only revealed what she wanted me to know. I regularly went back to Seattle to check on her, including conversations with neighbors. They gave me a clearer picture of her activities.

Many of these people knew me all my life, having played with their sons and daughters while growing up. To these longtime friends, I was not referred to with formality or unfamiliarity. I was not "Rev", as the people at one Fitness Center called me. I was not S. Robert Maddox. I was not even Bob. To them, I was *Bobby*. When my wife first heard me called by that name, her perspective changed. My South Dakota bride knew me as an Air Force Staff Sergeant, and as someone preparing for church ministry. She suddenly realized that I was once a little boy.

Jesus had just completed doing highly successful ministry in Capernaum and returned to his hometown of Nazareth. Entering His childhood synagogue, He attempted to help longstanding neighbors better understand freedom from sin, healing of diseases, and deliverance from oppression. Instead of being greeted with wonder, He was treated with hostility.

The proverbial statement, "Familiarity breeds contempt," is verified in this story. Intimacy should breed admiration but often raises scorn. Someone can become so well-known that people fail to appreciate, recognize, and acknowledge their special qualities.

What offends people about Jesus, and what happens when they choose to be offended?

What offends people about Jesus?

His message created a major stir among those who knew Him best. Comments were filled with sarcasm. Lifelong acquaintances responded disparagingly.

Cynicism is a cancer of the spirit—the bad cells of disdain attack the good cells of admiration and, if undiagnosed, eventually destroy hope.

The general opinion was that a common laborer was now parading about as a learned teacher. The most disturbing statement was, "Isn't this Mary's son…?"

Culturally, even if already deceased (as considered the case with Joseph) a man was known by the father. The comment "son of Mary" infers a rumor circulating that Jesus was illegitimate. Many knowing Him best gave substance to unfavorable and hurtful gossip about Mary and the family.

The more they talked amongst themselves, the more irritated and offended they became. With the message being irrefutable, the cynics attacked His reputation.

Why was the ministry of Jesus rejected?

First, His message does not conform to conventional wisdom. Jesus spoke about *grace* in a society of strict law, about *mercy* among people accustomed to revenge, and about *forgiveness* in a culture suppressed by a hated enemy. A compassionate message of love went against deeply ingrained prejudices.

"For the word of the cross is folly to those who are perishing, but to us who are being saved it is the power of God. For it is written, 'I will destroy the wisdom of the wise, and the discernment of the discerning I will thwart.' Where is the one who is wise? Where is the scribe? Where is the debater of this age? Has not God made foolish the wisdom of the world? For since, in the wisdom of God, the world did not know God through wisdom, it pleased God through the folly of what we preach to save those who believe. For Jews demand signs and Greeks seek wisdom, but we preach Christ crucified, a stumbling block to Jews and folly to Gentiles, but to those who are called, both Jews and Greeks, Christ the power of God and the wisdom of God. For the foolishness of God is wiser than men, and the weakness of God is stronger than men." (1 Corinthians 1:18-25)

A Supreme Court Justice, speaking at a prayer breakfast, emphasized that Christians are destined to be regarded as fools in modern society—fools for Christ's sake, needing the courage to endure the scorn of a sophisticated world. Intellectuals through history have rejected miracles, choosing to not investigate such things out of unbelief.

Disallowing miracles are irrational. You can be sophisticated and believe in God. Reason and intellect are clearly linked to faith.

Secondly, His ministry will not conform to faithless perceptions. People without faith treat spiritual matters lightly.

A radio personality known for acting raunchy on the air became angry by the number of postcards asking him to refrain from such behavior. During a program, he faked conversion to an elderly grandmother who had sent a card. He tried to get some money from her and she became suspicious. He pressured her, "Why can't you send a donation? Are you cheaping out on Jesus? Can't you cough up a ten-dollar bill? I just had a big conversion and now you're not sending me a dime. You better send cash or I'm going back to Satan." He treated the sacred contemptuously.

If God does not conform to selfish perceptions, or fit into falsely conceived patterns, faithless people are repulsed and offended by Jesus.

What happens when people are offended?

Simply this: Life altering manifestations of God do not occur in an atmosphere of sarcasm and cynicism. In the presence of expectancy, the poorest of human effort sees tremendous spiritual results.

On Father's Day, 1995, a burden for more of God's presence increased in a Florida church. Large numbers started attending services, many became devoted followers of Jesus, some were radically transformed. Out of deep-seated hunger for God, people came from all over the world. The sense of anticipation by those in attendance enhanced spiritual stirrings.

The unusual nature of activities caused controversy both in and out of the church community. Some behavior was divinely inspired, others were human responses needing guidance and instruction. Cynicism and sarcasm started coming from church leaders, those most familiar with Jesus.

ACTION

In an environment of critical coldness or bland indifference, the most Spirit-packed utterance falls lifeless to the ground. If people come together to hate, they hate. If people are determined to be unreasonable, they are difficult. If people are closed-minded, they never understand. However, if people gather to love Jesus and value each other, they experience God. Those knowing Jesus best can widely open or shut out the miraculous, they can help or hinder.

A guy approached a cab driver in New York and said, "Take me to London, England." The cab driver told him it was impossible to drive across the Atlantic. The customer insisted there was a way. "Drive me down to the pier and put the taxi on a freighter. When we get to Liverpool, drive me to London and I'll pay whatever is on the meter." The driver agreed. When they arrived in London, good to his word, the passenger paid the total on the meter plus a thousand-dollar tip.

The driver began roaming around London, not knowing what to do. A Londoner hailed him and said, "I want you to drive me to New York." The cab driver thought to himself, "What luck! How often can you pick up a fare in London wanting to go to New York?" As the passenger was describing how this could be done, the driver interrupted, "I know how to get to New York, but where do you want to go in New York?" The passenger said, "Riverside Drive and 104th Street." The driver responded, "Sorry, I don't go to the Westside!" and drove away.

What about you? Do you slam the door on God because of not liking everything you hear, or what is being asked of you? Do you refuse to go "to the Westside" and leave offended? Your attitude can be the reason why many wonderful blessings are failing to happen.

ACTION

People get offended because His message does not conform to conventional wisdom, and His ministry will not conform to faithless perceptions. Limited manifestations of the Spirit occur when people choose to be offended.

Jesus stated in the Sermon on the Mount: "Do not throw your pearls to pigs." (Matthew 7:6) Do not expect faith-filled efforts to be valued by faithless cynics. The message and ministry of Jesus are highly controversial. Those receptive to God will witness the power that is able to meet needs.

Create an atmosphere of expectancy. Jesus wants to manifest His supernatural nature. He declared what He can do; what will you allow?

CHAPTER EIGHT

REST

And he called the twelve and began to send them out two by two, and gave them authority over the unclean spirits. ... So they went out and proclaimed that people should repent. And they cast out many demons and anointed with oil many who were sick and healed them. ... The apostles returned to Jesus and told him all that they had done and taught. And he said to them, "Come away by yourselves to a desolate place and rest a while." For many were coming and going, and they had no leisure even to eat. And they went away in the boat to a desolate place by themselves. (Mark 6:7, 12-13,30-32)

In almost four decades of church ministry, hard work was never an issue. I cannot recall a time when I did only one job. A six-day work week was very normal; numerous weeks were without days off. On three separate occasions, I did not take a single vacation-day in an entire year, some years involved only one week.

Feeling indispensable was not the issue. Vacations sometimes required working twice as hard before going or twice as hard after returning. Occasionally, the momentary demands were so overwhelming less stress seemed involved just staying home; leaving was too much of a bother. Eventually, I had an emotional breakdown.

In almost every profession, people feel the mandate to be a high achiever—an inward pressure to constantly produce meaningful results. God is not necessarily pleased with this kind of mentality. A hustle-bustle way of life can dictate an unhealthy assertive mindset.

Many civilizations do not have a *hurry* viewpoint. Slower-pace cultures can be frustrating. In Guam, I almost starved waiting for a meal. In Okinawa, a spontaneous baseball game shut down an entire construction site. I asked a worker, "How does anything ever get done?" He replied, "What's the rush? It will be here tomorrow." In other words, why do today what can be done tomorrow?

What is often referred to as *leisure time* in America is far from relaxing and would be better called *discretionary time*. Weekends are quickly becoming busier than weekdays. Resting and experiencing relaxation is becoming a lost art.

While overseeing a Bible College, a school year ended with feelings of exhaustion. My wife and I decided to take a weekend trip. Reservations were made at the Relax Inn. After checking into the hotel, we found an out-of-way place to eat and decided to retire early the first night. The bed was hard, and the pillow was flat, producing restless sleep. The alarm clock was accidentally not turned off and we were startled awake early the next morning. Twenty-four hours later a fire alarm went off while dressing for the day, requiring us to walk down six floors of stairs, vacate the building and stand in the rain. Although scheduled to spend another night, we decided to check out. The Relax Inn was not very relaxing.

The disciples were sent on a mission and returned having experienced highly successful and effective ministry. Great results were achieved, and adrenaline was in overdrive, which converts into *down* feelings afterward. The body and mind need to recover.

In a culture much slower than today, Jesus showed concern for them needing rest. They returned from an assignment fired up. Instead of fanning the flames of enthusiasm, He cooled their jets. They were not challenged to do more, nor were they motivated to stay excited and continue moving in high gear. Rather than pumping them up, He pulled the plug, deflating the ego.

The disciples were part of a strategy that was producing dynamic outcomes. They saw a winning program, something worth reproducing. A good program can take precedent over its intended use. When an approach takes center stage and knowing Jesus becomes secondary, time away is required for gaining a renewed perspective. Programs can lose their intended purpose and only continue to work if the workers maintain mustered-up excitement.

Do you need rest? Are you failing to have a weekly restful day? Is your weekend filled with a different but equally exhausting activity? Jesus shows His disciples how to gain a renewed perspective and a revitalized life.

"Come with me."

Jesus does not say, "Go away," but "Come with me!" The Lord needs to be included. You are to remove yourself from places needing constant attention, places where distractions interrupt time with God.

Early in ministry, I went to the church office intending to start the day with prayer and meditation. Once arriving, however, things on my desk distracted me and time with God was pushed aside.

My personal time with Jesus is now done early each morning at home, at a time and location when nothing else gets my attention. Where do you go to come away with the Lord? It need not be far, just far enough for Him to have all your attention. It need not be long, just long enough for Him to renew your perspective.

While employed at a bank, one of my responsibilities involved distribution and mailing. At a time when postage was 8 cents an ounce, the postage budget was $30,000 a month. A secretary took the register each month and reconciled the department records with the amount of postage in the meter. Occasionally, the ledger would not balance, and she spent an excessive amount of time studying accounts. Out of frustration, she would ask me for help. A quick glance at the register often revealed the problem. She was so close to the situation she could not see obvious errors.

During difficulty, distance gives the ability to spot discrepancies and gain answers. Take a recess and separate yourself from the problems of life.

"By yourselves to a quiet place."

The place of renewal is in solitude, increasingly contrary to modern day lifestyles. People rarely go anywhere alone (not meaning another person). Visit a community park and observe sitters, walkers, and joggers, either by themselves or in a group, with personal electronic devices. A generation has risen afraid of silence. Are they fearful of what they might hear?

Noise robs communication with God, and the ability to clearly hear His voice. Quietness is required. The place of rest is a lonely place, without interference. Scripture declares, "Be still and know I am God."

A group of men went with their pastor on a fishing expedition to the Yukon. They loaded supplies, drove into Canada as far north as possible, and took a pontoon plane to an isolated lake. The vehicles were left in such a remote area that no static could be heard on the radio while turning the dial.

You are created needing alone places with the Lord, places without annoying static. In solitude, you can see yourself solely in relationship to Him, where the purpose of your life can be refined.

"Get some rest."

Resting does not mean forever lying in a hammock, something associated more with laziness. Rest involves three things:

Healthy food. Outlook is influenced by what you eat. Heavy doses of sugar and fatty foods do not lend themselves to mental rest.

Physical exercise. A rapid flow of blood cleans out toxins influencing feelings. Exercise makes the heart pump faster, the lungs breathe harder, and restores rested emotions. You gain a more wholesome point of view.

Sound sleep. Slumber clears confusion and lifts fog preventing a clear perspective. You are designed to dream, which only comes while sleeping.

My parents had a vacation place on Washington State's Olympic Peninsula, located near Diamond Point at Discovery Bay, just off the Strait of Juan de Fuca. The location was beautiful and away from everything. At night, the lights of Victoria, British Columbia were visible across the Strait—a picturesque setting.

When my father was close to retirement, he and my mother thought about changing their permanent residence from Seattle to their vacation property. In preparation, they started spending longer intervals at the place. Although great for brief stays, the site was very inconvenient as the primary residence. They sold the property and did more traveling.

Rest stops are seasonal retreats, not meant to

become permanent havens. Push the *pause* button occasionally, but do not drop out of the race. Rest is designed for only short intervals.

ACTION

Come away with the Lord to a place of solitude, go alone, and return with renewed perspectives and greater dedication. "They who wait for the LORD shall renew their strength; they shall mount up with wings like eagles; they shall run and not be weary; they shall walk and not faint." (Isaiah 40:31)

Allow yourself *waiting* time and experience rest in the Lord.

CHAPTER NINE

TRADITIONS

And the Pharisees and the scribes asked him, "Why do your disciples not walk according to the tradition of the elders, but eat with defiled hands?" And he said to them, "Well did Isaiah prophesy of you hypocrites, as it is written, "'This people honors me with their lips, but their heart is far from me; in vain do they worship me, teaching as doctrines the commandments of men.' You leave the commandment of God and hold to the tradition of men." And he said to them, "You have a fine way of rejecting the commandment of God in order to establish your tradition! For Moses said, 'Honor your father and your mother'; and, 'Whoever reviles father or mother must surely die.' But you say, 'If a man tells his father or his mother, "Whatever you would have gained from me is Corban"' (that is, given to God)—then you no longer permit him to do anything for his father or mother, thus making void the word of God by your tradition that you have handed down. And many such things you do." (Mark 7:5-13)

Mark 7 records several events rich in spiritual application. In one incident, Jesus says *things* are not primarily clean or unclean; impurity is the product of the heart. He next spoke forcibly about evil intentions, producing sins against God, others, and oneself. He then took issue with improper, hurtful, and destructive comments.

The chapter also shows the message of hope and grace is not only a Jewish experience. They had the first opportunity, but God's kingdom is designed for all people groups.

The chapter further demonstrates there is no uniform way for healing. Although difficult to understand the significance of fingers in ears and saliva on the tongue, handicaps and illnesses are different and so are healings. Jesus has an anointing custom designed for every need.

Of special interest is the discourse addressing traditions. Traditions are customs passed on to following generations, which can be good or bad.

The Christmas celebration in my home includes

a cherished memory from my Pacific Northwest upbringing. The holiday meal begins with a shrimp and crab cocktail, a custom producing wonderful feelings of treasured moments.

Traditions can also lose meaning and become useless. A little girl watched her mother prepare a ham and noticed she cut off the end before placing it in the roaster. She asked her mother why and was told, "Because grandma does it this way." Her grandmother came to dinner and the little girl asked, "Grandma, why do you cut off the end of the ham before placing it in the roaster?" She replied, "My mother does it this way." Her great-grandmother also came to dinner and the little girl asked, "Great-grandma, why do you cut off the end of the ham before placing it in the roaster?" She said, "Because my roaster is not big enough for the ham."

Do your spiritual traditions aid or hinder your life and vitality?

Traditions have good intentions

Traditions help people remember important truths, producing firm footing and stability. The Pharisees talking to Jesus would make any mother proud, washing hands before eating is good. You can never minimize the importance of proper hygiene.

Traditions can teach a truth or replace a truth.

How many people identify with a local church out of tradition instead of a relationship? Some refer to a church because of family connections, having little to do with active faith.

A hospital called my office about a woman being admitted claiming affiliation with the church. Not recognizing the name, I went to investigate. She was as surprised seeing me as I was meeting her. Her grandparents attended years earlier and the family called the church their own ever since.

Many church members attend services only monthly, others yearly. A joke states a person decided to quit attending church because the same songs were always sung: "Silent Night" and "Christ Arose." Going to services merely on Christmas and Easter is strictly a tradition.

One of the more notable sources of Christian tradition is advent and lent. On Ash Wednesday, soot from burned Palm branches is applied to the forehead, reminding people a spiritual lesson. Unfortunately, some consider the yearly practice the substance of grace.

A true story: A priest in Paris was being robbed. When the thief noticed his clergy collar, he decided not to rob him. Relieved the priest offered the would-be robber a cigar. The thief said, "No thanks, Father, I've given up smoking for Lent." How about giving up robbing for Jesus? Lent did not do much to change the thief's heart.

A man once said to me, "I'm a Lutheran first and a Christian second!" Tradition overcame conviction.

I gave oversight to a church in a very religious part of Minnesota. Townships such as the German community of Tracy, the Belgium community of Ghent, the Polish community of Ivanhoe were founded on old world customs and regularly celebrated their religious heritage.

A local minister loaned me his Psalter—a collection of Scripture readings devoted to dutiful worship. The book contains several virtuous truths. Many people earnestly performing traditional sacred practices are lacking a meaningful and vibrant relationship with God.

Traditions are not the exclusive property of liturgical churches. Spirit-filled believers also have traditions. In earlier years, Pentecostals usually began each church service with three songs, accompanied by piano and organ: an upbeat gospel song, a joyous testimonial song, and a slower redemption song. Ministers were against wearing clerical robes but eventually established dark suits with red ties as standard attire.

New traditions with regards to music style and

platform apparel are presently in-the-making; worship music must now be guitar driven and attire must be casual.

Inviting people to come to the front of an auditorium as an expression of faith is often referred to as a public confession. The practice was started in 1817 by Asahael Nettleton and popularized by Charles Finney. The Biblical confession of faith is water baptism, given less emphasis and not experienced by many new believers because of the traditional altar call.

The baptism in the Holy Spirit was initially highlighted weekly in worship gatherings but is now given emphasis mostly on Pentecost Sunday—seven weeks after Easter. The annual topic, if mentioned, often addresses *purpose* more than *experience*. The blessing is usually relegated to small group settings and summer camps and is increasingly neglected. Believers are being robbed of the benefit.

God has no grandchildren, only sons and daughters. Spirit baptism must be experienced fresh and anew by every generation. The fresh outpouring on Pentecost in Acts 2 must become a fresh downpour in the 21st Century.

Identity based on past practices is rooted in ritual, not reality. Churches saturated with tradition lose significance.

The mission of the church is not maintaining programs. Every denomination and movement have religious ruts and members are quick to grumble when their comfort zone is challenged. Many enriching activities have been continued without asking if they should be a one-time or short-lived experience? Most religious groups do not know when or how to end something losing relevance.

The Church went through the Church Growth era, emphasizing everyone a member, the Church Health era, emphasizing everyone a minister, and the Missional Church era, emphasizing everyone a missionary to their world of influence. God is progressively bringing the church to a predetermined end. The goal is not preserving the status quo, but advancement.

How do traditions get started?

Spiritual activities become traditions when actions are done *for* Christ rather than *in* Christ—when thinking, "Look what I'm doing *for* Jesus!" However, following Jesus is primarily a relationship, not activities.

You are a follower of Jesus by inviting Him into your life. You go through water baptism as a testimony of being in Christ. You become baptized in the Holy Spirit by living in Christ. You participate in communion as a testimony of abiding in Christ.

Nothing is done *for* Christ; everything is done *in* Christ. In Christ is reality; what is done for Christ is routine.

The Apostle Paul knew firsthand the power of tradition. "And I was advancing in Judaism beyond many of my own age among my people, so extremely zealous was I for the traditions of my fathers." (Galatians 1:14) He then discovered that meaningfulness comes only to a person that lives *in* Christ: "He … set me apart … called me by his grace … revealing his Son in me…." (Galatians 1:15-16)

Having your focus *in Christ* keeps purpose in religious routines, and helps critical spiritual disciplines stay fresh and life-changing.

When do traditions become a problem?

When repeated actions are a *burden* and no longer a *blessing*, traditions become *barriers*. Initially, various activities often cause a sense of closeness to God but can easily slip into a meaningless obligation.

Should the practice be thrown out? The problem is not the routine. Jesus must once again invade your spiritual habits and become the focal point of your energies.

Jesus shut within a Book

Is hardly worth a passing look;
Jesus shut within a creed
Is a fruitless Lord indeed.
But Jesus in the hearts of men
Shows His tenderness again.
(Gordon Grooms)

Daily prayers, Scripture reading, and regularly gathering with believers can either be traditions of meaningless boredom or blessings of unlimited measure. Renew abiding *in* Christ, instead of doing *for* Christ.

"Who has bewitched you? It was before your eyes that Jesus Christ was publicly portrayed as crucified. Let me ask you only this: Did you receive the Spirit by works of the law or by hearing with faith? Are you so foolish? Having begun by the Spirit, are you now being perfected by the flesh?" (Galatians 3:1-3)

ACTION

Beware of making *sacred cows* out of *spiritual customs*. Be constantly on guard of becoming bound by traditions. The endeavors of the spiritual life are not the problem. The problem is *living in activities* rather than *lingering in Christ*—both have the power to possess. Activities can bring bondage, while Jesus will bring liberty.

CHAPTER TEN

WONDER-WHAT-WOW

In those days, when again a great crowd had gathered, and they had nothing to eat, he called his disciples to him and said to them, "I have compassion on the crowd, because they have been with me now three days and have nothing to eat. And if I send them away hungry to their homes, they will faint on the way. And some of them have come from far away." And his disciples answered him, "How can one feed these people with bread here in this desolate place?" And he asked them, "How many loaves do you have?" They said, "Seven." And he directed the crowd to sit down on the ground. And he took the seven loaves, and having given thanks, he broke them and gave them to his disciples to set before the people; and they set them before the crowd. And they had a few small fish. And having blessed them, he said that these also should be set before them. And they ate and were satisfied. And they took up the broken pieces left over, seven baskets full. ... And Jesus, aware of this, said to them, "Why are you discussing the fact that you have no bread? Do you not yet perceive or understand? Are your hearts hardened? Having eyes do you not see, and having ears do you not hear? And do you not remember? When I broke the five loaves for the five thousand, how many baskets full of broken pieces did you take up?" They said to him, "Twelve." "And the seven for the four thousand, how many baskets full of broken pieces did you take up?" And they said to him, "Seven." And he said to them, "Do you not yet understand?" (Mark 8:1-8, 17-21)

The recorded scene was a great moment in the life of Jesus but led to a misunderstanding. When Jesus concluded feeding over four-thousand people, the Pharisees asked for a sign. He responded by groaning deeply. What more proof did they need? What would satisfy them? Their unappeasable hankering to constantly challenge His authenticity was blinding them from seeing the truth.

Jesus and the Twelve got into a boat. While crossing the Sea of Galilee, He mulled over the incident in His mind and suddenly gave a warning, "Be careful of the yeast of the Pharisees and of Herod." The disciples did not grasp the spiritual implications of the day's events. Jesus was pondering an altercation; they were preoccupied with food.

The symbolism of yeast in the Bible represents corruption: changing for the worse; wicked behavior; depravity; decay; rottenness.

Many distortions of life end with "*ism*". The yeast of Pharisees is *traditionalism*—bound to the past and binding people to routines and customs. The yeast of Herod is *secularism*—rationalism and pragmatism is what is right and beneficial.

Followers of Jesus are to guard against the penetrating effect of two corruptions: bondage to the past, and rationalizing substandard living. Spiritual manna becomes putrefied by these two harmful viruses. They permeate, afflict, and deprive believers of tasting the freshness of the Holy Spirit.

While the Twelve were kicking themselves for not bringing bread, Jesus sharpened their spiritual sensitivity through a rapid series of questions. He challenged them about being preoccupied with temporal things.

Spiritual focus looks beyond human existence. His message is about living eternally, not about helping sinful people feel better maintaining an unwholesome and substandard lifestyle.

Jesus was not satisfied with the Twelve only remembering events but wanted them to recall details. What are some applications?

No pattern exists in miracles

His questions remind the Twelve that five loaves fed five thousand and seven loaves fed four thousand. The disciples also noticed it took five loaves to produce twelve baskets of leftovers and seven loaves to produce seven baskets.

No rhyme-to-reason was shown between the requirement and the result. Logically, if five loaves fed five thousand, then only four loaves are needed to feed four thousand. Rationally, if five loaves produced twelve baskets of leftovers, then seven loaves should produce sixteen baskets. Yet, more product produced less results. Where is the efficiency?

People naturally look for logical progressions: patterns that develop principles; similarities that devise formulas. Peace of mind is often connected to everything moving sequentially and orderly. Successful ventures supposedly occur only by developing strategies and systems. An age-old motto reads, "Those who fail to plan, plan to fail."

But miracles cannot be calculated or duplicated. They work outside the normal rudiments of life. A miracle is like a Pinocchio—something extraordinary happening without strings attached.

Do you believe God is always systematic and predictable? In some ways, yes! He always responds mercifully to repentance. Miracles, however, dwell outside the realm of measurable things and are impossible to define.

A man was walking his dog on a beach when he came upon another beachcomber. The proud owner of the dog said, "Watch this!" and tossed a piece of driftwood into the sea. The dog immediately ran on top of the water, fetched the wood and ran back. The visitor shook his head in disbelief. The owner repeated the act two more times and asked the person, "Did you notice anything unusual?" The guy responded, "Yeah, your dog can't swim, can he?"— a rational response to an unexplainable occurrence.

God moving in miraculous ways leads to *wonder*, a feeling beyond scrutiny and measurement. What comes first, a sense of wonder that produces miracles, or miracles that produce wonder? Hard to answer with any sense of certainty!

Are you suspiciously assessing the supernatural and, like Pharisees, refusing to recognize signs and wonders? Have you lost the simplicity of faith that enhances wonder? God still works mysteriously and miraculously.

Give what you have

A common factor between feeding five thousand and four thousand was the Twelve using what was available and in their possession. On both occasions, Jesus asked the same question, word for word, "How many loaves do you have?" His disciples may have picked up on the inquiry, their minds registering, "We've heard this before!"

Jesus is still asking His followers, "*What* do you have? What will you give to effectively address the need of the moment?"

An important truth about stewardship is considering possessions something entrusted to you and always available to the Lord. Stewards understand possessions are a privilege, not a right. The parable of talents, recorded in Matthew 25, reveals stewards know *responsibility* is paramount to *privilege*. Everyone is a steward entrusted with a portion of His world, having responsibility and the privilege to faithfully manage. What you have is God's gift to you; what you make of it is your gift to God.

Stewards manage things under their care. Part of divine management involves tithing, giving ten percent of earnings to advance the message of grace and hope. Tithing is *rent* for the use of His possessions, and testifies His Lordship over a lifestyle. The money earned is not your own but is entrusted to you for proper disbursement.

Giving does not end at ten percent. Living by *grace* instead of *law*, ten percent is the beginning point. Out of obedience and faith, why not give twenty percent or more?

Do not believe for a moment that you will start giving when you can better afford it. Giving larger amounts is developed when having only smaller earnings. If you are not trustworthy with a little, you cannot be entrusted with more.

Everything in your home is either an idol or a tool. How do you view the possessions under your care?

Little is much when God is involved

Jesus was concerned that people might collapse from hunger on their way home. He wanted the Twelve to feed four thousand with seven loaves.

The relationship between the assignment and the resource was not proportional. If an equal amount of available bread was allocated to each person, everyone would receive a crumb, hardly enough to address malnourishment.

Do you underestimate what can be accomplished with little amounts? An angel said to

Mary with regards to the divine conception, "For nothing is impossible with God." (Luke 1:57) Jesus responded to someone underestimating His ability by saying, "Everything is possible for him who believes." (Mark 9:23)

Are you misjudging God? Are you putting limitations on what He can do through you? A familiar motto reads, "The only ability God wants is availability."

ACTION

Live with wonder, what and wow:

Wonder: miracles do not fit into systems and formulas. Gain a sense of wonder about the supernatural workings of God.

What: the Lord still asks His followers, "What do you have?" Give generously!

Wow: do not underestimate what God can do through you.

CHAPTER ELEVEN
CONSEQUENCES

"Whoever causes one of these little ones who believe in me to sin, it would be better for him if a great millstone were hung around his neck and he were thrown into the sea. And if your hand causes you to sin, cut it off. It is better for you to enter life crippled than with two hands to go to hell, to the unquenchable fire. And if your foot causes you to sin, cut it off. It is better for you to enter life lame than with two feet to be thrown into hell. And if your eye causes you to sin, tear it out. It is better for you to enter the kingdom of God with one eye than with two eyes to be thrown into hell, 'where their worm does not die and the fire is not quenched.' For everyone will be salted with fire. Salt is good, but if the salt has lost its saltiness, how will you make it salty again? Have salt in yourselves, and be at peace with one

another." (Mark 9:42-50)

Years ago, I went to the Illinois Governor's Prayer Breakfast at the Hyatt Regency O'Hare. Former Missouri Governor John Ashcroft spoke about consequences. One of his more memorable comments was, "In America, we perceive freedom as living without consequences but that is not freedom; that is meaninglessness."

In life, there are consequences to everything, described in the Bible as reaping what is sowed. *Good* consequences come as *benefits* or *rewards*, and *bad* consequences come as *justice* or *punishment*. A phrase written in the margin of my Bible says, "Act first, think second, regret forever!" Poor actions, based on mindless decisions, lead to unpleasant consequences.

Jesus spoke of bad decisions, unquenchable consequences, and purity.

Ensnaring others

The warning about "little ones" is twofold: The *first* application applies to children: "Whoever causes one of these little ones who believe in me to sin, it would be better for him if a great millstone were hung around his neck and he were thrown into the sea." Mark 9:42 is related to Mark 9:36-37: "He took a child and put him in the midst of them, and taking him in his arms, he said to them, 'Whoever receives one such child in my name receives me, and whoever receives me, receives not me but him who sent me.'" Children have a natural instinct to learn, and constantly observe what others do.

A minister baptized a new believer one Sunday and concluded by saying, "In the name of the Father, and in the Son, and in the Holy Ghost." Afterward, he and his family were invited to a home in the country. The children went outside to play.

After a while, there was only silence and the parents wondered what the children were up to. They found them behind the barn quietly playing church. The four-year-old was conducting a baptismal service. With a cat suspended over a barrel of water, and trying to be as solemn as her father, she repeated the phrase she heard, "I baptize you in the name of the Father, and in the Son, and into the hole you go!"

Following Jesus involves positively influencing the lives of children, praying and actively inspiring them with the love of God. Older generations should seek meaningful times with younger generations: talking, shaping, motivating, encouraging.

The *second* application relates to new believers, those young in the Lord. Paul wrote to the Corinthian church, "So, whether you eat or drink, or whatever you do, do all to the glory of God. Give no offense to

Jews or to Greeks or to the church of God, just as I try to please everyone in everything I do, not seeking my own advantage, but that of many, that they may be saved. Be imitators of me, as I am of Christ." (1 Corinthians 10:31-11:1)

Causing the most obscure, insignificant, or weak follower of Jesus to stumble carries serious consequences. Be careful attempting to justify behavior by thinking: "Wrong for you; okay for me!" What kind of attitude is that? Does it enhance God's kingdom? Live an exemplary life, in ways others can emanate.

Being cast into a sea with a large millstone attached around the neck would be better than hindering others from closely connecting with Jesus. An agonizing physical death is preferable to being a stumbling block to others. To sin is terrible, to teach another to sin is infinitely worse. The consequence impacts personal survival.

In a fable about a little girl whose mother died, dad came home from work, sat down, took off his jacket, lit his pipe and put his feet on a footstool. Out of loneliness, the little girl asked him to play but he wanted to be left alone. He told her to go play in the street. She played in the streets and eventually took to the streets.

Years later, she died. Her soul arrived at heaven

and Peter said to Jesus, "There's a girl standing at the door who was bad in her lifetime. I suppose we should send her straight to hell?" Jesus gently replied, "No, let her in." Then with stern eyes, He said, "But look for a man who refused to play with his little girl and sent her out into the streets. Send him to hell."

Although just an anecdote, the consequence is more demanding on anyone making it easier for others to sin, whose thoughtless or deliberate conduct puts a stumbling block in the path of impressionable minds and weaker believers.

Ensnaring yourself

The hand, foot, and eye are three body parts that produce behavior, none act independently of the heart. The hand refers to *action*; the foot refers to *placement*; the eye refers to *watch*.

If what you do, where you go, and what you see is corrupt and unwholesome, radical surgery is needed by the Supreme Surgeon. The amputation should be immediate and decisive. No halfway measure will suffice or you will bleed to death. Just as eliminating a body part is sometimes the only way to preserve human life, removing activities, places, and sights may be necessary to preserve eternal life. Heart issues jeopardize eternity.

The street called Wayward is a roadway leading to destruction. The word "hell" is the Biblical term "Gehenna," coming from the word *Hinnom*—a ravine just outside of Jerusalem with an evil past and sad history. King Ahaz instituted fire worship and sacrificed little children in the valley. Scripture states he "burned his sons as an offering." (2 Chronicles 28:3) King Manasseh also roasted children to death to the idol Molech in this valley. The place gives testimony of a terrible lapse into heathen customs.

Eventually, the valley was considered unclean and became the garbage dump of Jerusalem. Refuse continually burned, and smoke rose out of a vast incinerator. The place reveals that consequences for evil behavior are foul and loathsome.

Hell is described as having two destroying forces, one inward and one outward. The internal destroyer is worm-breeding guilt slowly eating away the last aspect of life; the external destroyer is unquenchable fire. Hell is a horrible fate, a combination of inherent pains of shame eating within and indescribable punishment inflicted without. To avoid this retributive consequence is worth any sacrifice, any discipline, and any amount of personal denial.

Only in obedience to God is there a life that ultimately ends with satisfying peace. Eternity necessitates expunging destructive habits, abandoning unwholesome pleasures, giving up harmful relationships, and cutting out objectionable possessions.

Is there anything in your life standing between you and perfect obedience to God? Root it out! The removal may be as painful as a surgical procedure and feel like a vital part is being severed. Although thought as extreme, harsh, and stern, some things must be eliminated.

Purifying salt

Salt was added to sacrifices before offered on an altar of fire, making it acceptable. Fire has two connotations: *destruction* (an ungodly lifestyle destroyed by the purifying fire of God's mercy), and *refinement* (a lifestyle made precious by the preserving fire of God's grace).

"In this you rejoice, though now for a little while, if necessary, you have been grieved by various trials, so that the tested genuineness of your faith—more precious than gold that perishes though it is tested by fire—may be found to result in praise and glory and honor at the revelation of Jesus Christ. (1 Peter 1:6-7)

The hardships of life are a refining fire. Sorrows season your sacrifice and strengthen your purity. The salt of suffering brings about refinement.

As society shows signs of corruption, followers of Jesus are to be an antibiotic. Actively combat evil viruses causing deadly infections. Aggressively destroy contaminating influences.

Society is also showing indifference toward consequences. Luxuries and excess are driving people to careless thrills. From restless stirrings, many live in temporal extremes. Followers of Jesus are to impart a thirst for eternity that is greater than momentary and passing pleasures.

Society needs the dynamic influence of faithful and pure followers of Christ. When believers squabble over greatness, pursue self-gratification, and act with prejudice toward others, they no longer serve as a cleansing solution and seasoning agent. Instead, the church blandly blends in with others.

ACTION

Ensnaring others is quicksand and ensnaring yourself is thin ice, both lead to ruin.

An Indiana cemetery has a tombstone (more than a hundred years old) that bears the following epitaph:

"Pause Stranger, when you pass me by,
As you are now, so once was I

ACTION

As I am now, so you will be,
So prepare for death and follow me."

An unknown passerby read those words and underneath scratched this reply:

"To follow you I'm not content,
Until I know which way you went."

Watch where you lead others and watch where you go.

The Holy Spirit has come to help you spotlessly abide in Christ, purifying you of bitterness, anger, and grudge-bearing. He can clean out moodiness, irritability, and selfishness—chronic issues growing increasingly problematic. Life is wholesome and abundant when emptied of self-centeredness and filled with Christ-servitude.

CHAPTER TWELVE

BARTIMAEUS

And they came to Jericho. And as he was leaving Jericho with his disciples and a great crowd, Bartimaeus, a blind beggar, the son of Timaeus, was sitting by the roadside. And when he heard that it was Jesus of Nazareth, he began to cry out and say, "Jesus, Son of David, have mercy on me!" And many rebuked him, telling him to be silent. But he cried out all the more, "Son of David, have mercy on me!" And Jesus stopped and said, "Call him." And they called the blind man, saying to him, "Take heart. Get up; he is calling you." And throwing off his cloak, he sprang up and came to Jesus. And Jesus said to him, "What do you want me to do for you?" And the blind man said to him, "Rabbi, let me recover my sight." And Jesus said to him, "Go your way; your faith has made you well." And immediately he recovered his sight and followed him on the way. (Mark 10:46-52)

Just before the Passover, Jesus is traveling to Jerusalem. Having gone through Jericho, located a few miles north of the Dead Sea, He is about to ascend the steep hill toward the Holy City. The Jordan valley is busy with holiday travelers. Thousands are passing through, and beggars are vigorously seeking contributions. Sitting alongside the road is a man named Bartimaeus. He needs benevolence, either money or sight—he prefers sight.

Unusual stirrings develop as people pass the blind beggar. The murmuring of the crowd is different than normal. Many are eagerly attempting to get a glimpse of a Galilean who pitted Himself against the orthodoxy of the day. The man needing sight asks what is happening and is told the Miracle Worker from Nazareth is approaching.

Before the Son of God passes, the son of Timaeus takes extraordinary measures to get His attention, continually crying out, "Jesus, son of David, have mercy on me." The crowd tries to silence him, but this is an opportunity to escape a world of darkness. Other beggars want Jesus to notice them but Bartimaeus is more determined. He yells with such force and resolve that he gets the undivided attention of the Healer.

ACTION

If you want a special encounter with Jesus, take to heart the actions of Bartimaeus. He shows how to connect with Jesus in ways that meet needs.

Be persistent

Nothing stopped his clamoring. He was utterly and totally determined. He held firmly on course, was tenacious, and courageously different. The opposition did not deter him, he almost appeared stubborn. His need urged him to persist. This was more than a sentimental wish; he was desperate to experience Jesus' touch.

Various stories about the sight of others being restored may have created hope in his heart. News reports created a passion to believe God for his situation. People, today, still need to hear about individuals genuinely touched by Jesus, imparting hope and increasing determination to seek God for answers.

The first requirement for a miracle is sheer determination. Cry out to God with persistence, no matter the resistance. Actions reveal how much you want His attention.

Quickly come

When summoned by Jesus, he cast aside his coat and immediately came. The garment of comfort and security was taken off. Nothing was going to encumber him. He was decisive and immediate, without hesitation. Sincerity is seen by an eager response.

I developed a smoking habit prior to following Jesus, averaging a pack and a half of cigarettes a day. After asking Jesus to be my Lord and Savior, a sense of remorse developed about the addiction. The Bible speaks of the human body being the dwelling place of the Holy Spirit. No chemical dependency should rule behavior and destroy His temple. The conviction about quitting steadily increased.

Early in my relationship with God, an occasion occurred that caused me to go without tobacco for a few weeks, an opportunity to discard my source of comfort and security. There was absolutely no craving to smoke throughout the time. The Lord provided a gateway to quitting without nicotine withdrawal. Unfortunately, I resumed smoking at the first chance.

The conviction to quit smoking never stopped. I attempted to tune out the nagging in my soul, but feelings of guilt never left. A few years later, I was determined to finally quit. Ending the destructive dependency had every discomfort associated with withdrawal.

The opportunity to easily quit passed me by. A

miraculous moment came, but without eagerness and decisiveness the problem continued. Hesitation left me in bondage. Many opportunities only happen once, a second occasion may be more demanding.

Have you concluded an unwholesome habit or unhealthy vice should not be part of your life? Are you feeling a need to give yourself more fully to God? A common phrase states: "Strike while the iron is hot!" Act on the desire immediately. The environment may never be quite right again. When given a divine opportunity, make the most of the moment.

Be precise

The blind man knew what he wanted. His request was not ambiguous.

When visiting a doctor, a patient will ask for a definite symptom to receive attention. When visiting a dentist, a patient will ask for a certain tooth to be treated. Those looking for a miracle know what they need and should prayerfully ask Jesus to meet it. He is still saying, "What do you want Me to do for you?"

In the days of great cattle ranches, a little burro would sometimes be harnessed to a wild steed. Bucking and raging, the two would be turned loose to proceed out into the range. They could be seen disappearing over the horizon, the great steed dragging the little burro along and throwing him about. They would sometimes be gone for days but eventually would come back.

The little burro would be seen first, trotting back across the horizon and leading the submissive horse in tow. Somewhere out on the range, the stallion would become exhausted from trying to get rid of the burro and, in that moment, the burro would take control and become the leader.

In God's kingdom, the victory goes to the determined, not the outraged. Answers come to those asking specifically, not the melodramatic.

What do you desire from Him? Be crystal-clear in your request, only then will you know what to expect.

Have faith

The blind man considered Jesus simply a descendant of David, possibly the One leading the nation to political freedom. Faith made up the deficit in his understanding. Faith gave him spiritual insight. "Now faith is the assurance of things hoped for, the conviction of things not seen." (Hebrews 11:1) Spiritual vision led to the restoration of physical sight.

Miracles are not dependent upon fully grasping

God and His grace. You will never totally comprehend everything associated with Jesus. When unable to understand His actions clearly or completely, faith fills the shortfall.

Faith is more than intellectual assent. Faith believes with heart and will, with adoration and action. Faith is critical for meeting ongoing needs.

Be grateful

Having received sight, he did not selfishly go his way. He followed Jesus. Starting with a felt need, through thankfulness he experienced the answer to his genuine need.

There is a legend of a man who found the barn where the satan kept his seeds ready to be sown into the human heart. He discovered the seed of discouragement was more numerous than others and learned they could grow anywhere. When the devil was questioned further, the nemesis reluctantly admitted there was one place where he could never get them to grow: in the heart of grateful people.

Gratitude should be a lifestyle. People must guard against becoming more demanding and less thankful. Some act like a little boy who, on his return from a party, was asked by his mother, "Did you thank the host of the party?" He replied, "I was going to but the kid ahead of me said thank you and the lady said not to mention it, so I didn't."

When someone asks you for help, who do you desire to assist: someone thankful or unappreciative? Be sure to thank the Lord. Gratefully follow the One who miraculously meets your need.

ACTION

What do you need from Jesus? Provisions? Intervention? Healing? Restoration? The Lord who is the same yesterday, today, and forever is passing your way. Like Bartimaeus, be persistent, come quickly, be precise, have faith, and be grateful.

CHAPTER THIRTEEN

AUTHORITY

And they came again to Jerusalem. And as he was walking in the temple, the chief priests and the scribes and the elders came to him, and they said to him, "By what authority are you doing these things, or who gave you this authority to do them?" Jesus said to them, "I will ask you one question; answer me, and I will tell you by what authority I do these things. Was the baptism of John from heaven or from man? Answer me." And they discussed it with one another, saying, "If we say, 'From heaven,' he will say, 'Why then did you not believe him?' But shall we say, 'From man'?"—they were afraid of the people, for they all held that John really was a prophet. So they answered Jesus, "We do not know." And Jesus said to them, "Neither will I tell you by what authority I do these things." (Mark 11:27-33)

The Temple was cleared the day before of its official merchants, and religious leaders were upset with Jesus. Considering His actions unauthorized, they asked, "By what authority are you doing these things?" Asking the question differently: "Who put you in charge; where did you get consent; show me your permission slip?" Questions of authority are still asked today.

In the early 1900's, the church gained an increased awareness of the need to become full of the Holy Spirit. In the late 1960's, the church became much more receptive to spiritual gifts and afterward gave greater attention to *spiritual warfare*.

In the last days, prior to the Lord's return, the Holy Spirit will overflow from the lives of believers and the church will war against the evil one for the heart of the nations. Those following Jesus can expect spiritual conflict. A major focus in spiritual warfare is *authority*.

Words are an important part of life. Church leaders are *word* doctors, studying and using words to communicate His story and expecting them to be the catalyst of life-change. Is a word, rooted in the phrase "taking authority", causing confusion in the church? Anything suggesting *taking* is not conducive with a *giving* mindset—a primary component of abundant living. Scripture does not instruct followers of Jesus to take authority.

Living in a chaotic world, people want more control of their situations, to be in charge of their destiny and act authoritatively. Do you sometimes attempt to take authority and call it spiritual warfare? *Taking* suggests an unwillingness for God's will to be contrary to your wishes; *taking* lends itself to thinking God needs help. An unhealthy feeling attached to taking is impatience, which is not consistent with the fruit of the Spirit.

David found himself in a position where he could take the nation of Israel away from the less honorable King Saul. He was even counseled to take his life. The Spirit of the Lord, however, said to him, "You are not to *take* what I have not *given* you."

What is spiritual authority and how do believers fight spiritual battles?

Authority is invested in Jesus

Authority was given by the Heavenly Father to Jesus with a purpose: "As the Father has life in himself, so he has granted the Son also to have life in himself. And he has given him authority to execute judgment, because he is the Son of Man." (John 5:26-27)

With authority came instructions on its intended

use. Jesus said with regards to His life, "No one takes it from me, but I lay it down of my own accord. I have authority to lay it down, and I have authority to take it up again. This charge I have received from my Father." (John 10:18)

The sphere of His authority encompasses all mankind. When praying, Jesus said about Himself, "You have given him authority over all flesh, to give eternal life to all whom you have given him. (John 17:2)

Jesus demonstrated divine authority:

He spoke authoritatively: "…for he was teaching them as one who had authority, and not as their scribes." (Matthew 7:29).

He acted authoritatively: "But that you may know that the Son of Man has authority on earth to forgive sins"—he then said to the paralytic—"Rise, pick up your bed and go home." (Matthew 9:6)

Others recognized that He had authority: A military commander replied, "Lord, I am not worthy to have you come under my roof, but only say the word, and my servant will be healed. For I too am a man under authority, with soldiers under me." (Matthew 8:8-9)

Most important: Scripture reveals He possesses

an all-inclusive authority. Jesus declares in the Great Commission, "All authority in heaven and on earth has been given to me…." (Matthew 28:18)

The Father gave Jesus an everlasting authority, resting solely on Him and residing in Him. Out of His authority come acts of mercy and compassion. The truest characteristic of authority is not domination but the power to forgive and the means to release those who are captives. This world designs authority as a method to enslave—His authority brings freedom.

Authority is available by abiding in Jesus

There is no authority outside of a personal relationship with the *King of kings*. Acts 19 records, "Then some of the itinerant Jewish exorcists undertook to invoke the name of the Lord Jesus over those who had evil spirits, saying, 'I adjure you by the Jesus whom Paul proclaims.' Seven sons of a Jewish high priest named Sceva were doing this. But the evil spirit answered them, 'Jesus I know, and Paul I recognize, but who are you?' And the man in whom was the evil spirit leaped on them, mastered all of them and overpowered them, so that they fled out of that house naked and wounded." (Acts 19:13-16)

Authority is available to the extent that a person stays connected to Jesus. Why do believers naturally pray when bogged down in spiritual conflict? Prayer builds intimacy. The closer you are to Him, the greater His authority is witnessed in you and your struggle. Victory comes by drawing closer to Jesus.

A gospel writer recorded the story of a demon-possessed boy. (Mark 9) The disciples tried to cast out the demon and failed. Jesus arrived and set the boy free. The Twelve wondered, "Why couldn't we cast out the demon?" The answer is simple: There is no authority when Jesus is not present.

He later told them, "This kind can come out only by prayer." Prayer creates closeness. Without an ongoing intimate relationship with Jesus, no authority exists. Divine authority is in direct proportion to the relationship you develop with Him. By daily giving yourself to Christ, His authority governs the day.

Authority is experienced by yielding, by giving, and by submitting—actions Scripturally mandated to His followers. You do not have the means to dictate the best course of action but do have the ability to yield your circumstances to God.

In the Sermon on the Mount, Jesus teaches that if commanded to go one mile to add a second. The first mile is forcibly *taken*, the second mile is *given*, and His authority is manifested through your actions. Jesus also said if told to give a coat to include a shirt. The first is unavoidably *demanded*, the second is *submitted*, and His authority is witnessed over your possessions. His divine authority should influence every situation.

Rather than depend on individual might, rely on His strength. You are to abide in His authority. Take responsibility for your actions, yet decrease in self-reliance. Spiritual power is perfected in personal weakness. (2 Corinthians 12:9)

Authority is conditional to God's will

No authority exists outside of His plan. Jesus refers to mountains moving by faith. Complete the picture: If it is not God's will for a mountain to be relocated, it will not happen. You cannot act authoritatively over something contrary to God's intentions. He *gives* authority in line with His design.

To the extent that you act in accordance with His will, you have an authority to achieve it. God's blessing is not associated with anything you attempt to do on your own. You cannot do something with a hope of getting a divine seal of approval. All things are done in Christ, with the assurance that His purpose prevails.

One command directly associates Christ's authority with God's will: "All authority in heaven and on earth has been given to me. Go therefore and make disciples of all nations…." (Matthew 28:18-

19)

You presently have authority to tell the world about Jesus, later comes an authority to rule and reign. Presently, His followers are a crucible to the nations; very soon they will oversee them with resurrection power.

Give yourself to the nations until the day comes to rule by His authority. You have no right to rule nations until giving your life to reach them for Christ.

ACTION

Authority does not involve taking but *giving*; authority is invested in Jesus and is experienced by *abiding* in Him; spiritual authority comes by yielding and *submitting* your life to Christ; no authority exists outside His will.

In the city of Glasgow, Scotland, Helen Ewing decided to follow Jesus. She was described as "a slip of a girl." With Jesus as her absolute Lord, His anointing flowed from her. She had no outstanding personality, never wrote a book, and never composed a hymn. She was not a preacher and never traveled more than 200 miles from her home. She died at the age of 22. When she died, however, people wrote about her life.

She got up early every morning to read Scripture

and pray. She prayed for hundreds of missionaries. In one of her many diaries, 300 missionaries were listed. She had the date when she started a petition and when God answered. Her prayer life was powerful.

When she went on the campus of Glasgow University, her presence caused people to act better. If students were telling inappropriate stories and she approached, someone would say, "Quiet, Helen is coming." She unconsciously left the presence of God. Her life was a testimony of spiritual warfare and authority.

Authority comes by *giving* yourself more fully to Jesus.

S. ROBERT MADDOX

CHAPTER FOURTEEN

MOUNTAIN-MOVING PRAYERS

On the following day, when they came from Bethany, he was hungry. And seeing in the distance a fig tree in leaf, he went to see if he could find anything on it. When he came to it, he found nothing but leaves, for it was not the season for figs. And he said to it, "May no one ever eat fruit from you again." And his disciples heard it. ... As they passed by in the morning, they saw the fig tree withered away to its roots. And Peter remembered and said to him, "Rabbi, look! The fig tree that you cursed has withered." And Jesus answered them, "Have faith in God. Truly, I say to you, whoever says to this mountain, 'Be taken up and thrown into the sea,' and does not doubt in his heart, but believes that what he says will come to pass, it will be done for him. Therefore I tell you, whatever you ask in prayer, believe that you have received it, and it will be yours. And whenever you stand praying, forgive, if you have anything against anyone, so that your Father also who is in heaven may forgive you your trespasses." (Mark 11:12-14, 20-25)

This incident seems odd for two reasons: First, Jesus always refused to use miraculous powers for His own sake. In the wilderness, He would not satisfy hunger by turning stones into bread. He also did not call down heaven to escape the cross of Golgotha. What happened to the fig tree was not a *selfish* act!

Secondly, Mark explains this was not the season for figs. Why curse something for failing to do what normally does not occur? This was not a *punishing* act.

The leaves were a sign that Jesus could rightfully expect to find fruit. He was giving an enacted parable—a symbolic and dramatic action condemning *hypocrisy*. Jesus was symbolically demonstrating an unfulfilled promise: the tree was promising fruit but gave none.

Unfortunately, some lives can be summed up as lived in three stages: When young, it is said, *"They will do something!"* As they grow older, it is said, *"They can do something if they make the effort."* Towards the end, it is said, *"They might have done something had they tried."* Their lives showed promise but ended unfulfilled.

Jesus also dramatically illustrated a non-producing confession. The leafy tree was professing fruitfulness but not yielding a harvest. Not only is fruitlessness condemned, but also claiming fruitfulness when none existed.

Within a day, the formerly lush fig tree was completely dried up. The disciples were surprised at the withering speed. The tree was *fruitless* on the surface and *lifeless* in the roots. Uselessness invites disaster. Are non-producing believers actually dead and simply failing to show their true condition?

Jesus does not explain His actions but uses the event to emphasize faith. Unless faith in God makes you a better and more useful person, makes your home a more pleasant place to live, and makes your life sweeter for those around you, it is not faith at all. Entrance into the heavenly realm is by faithfully doing His will, not just piously crying, "Lord, Lord!"

The metaphor "mountain" has its setting in the Old Testament book of Zechariah. The leader Zerubbabel was facing insurmountable opposition rebuilding the temple. The prophet gave him an encouraging word: "Who are you, O great mountain? Before Zerubbabel you shall become a plain. And he shall bring forward the top stone amid shouts of 'Grace, grace to it!' ... The hands of Zerubbabel have laid the foundation of this house; his hands shall also complete it. Then you will know that the LORD of hosts has sent me to you." (Zechariah 4:7, 9)

Moving mountains is about facing overwhelming situations. What impossible circumstance are you dealing with right now? What kind of prayer bears fruit and produces an abundant harvest? Three attitudes create triumphant prayers.

Faith

Faith-filled prayers give access to problem-solving power, making possible overcoming capability. Faith involves a willingness to take problems to God. The real test of faith is, will you ask God for help?

There was a popular saying years ago, "Let go and let God!" Are you personally taking action that rightfully belongs to the Lord? Give up control and have the Lord rule over every situation. Nothing is too big or too small for Him.

Faith also involves being willing to accept divine guidance. Some ask for guidance when all they really want is approval for action already determined.

Pastors are not therapists. People coming for pastoral counseling can expect a prayerful listener,

ACTION

insight from Scripture, a guiding word from the Lord, and an encouraging Spirit-led prayer. Pastors attempt to be as kind as possible but speak the truth in love. When someone desires something inconsistent with Scripture, there is little room for approval, blessing, support, or sympathy. Foolishness cannot be sanctioned, and pastoral relationships often end up jeopardized.

Similarly, it is useless seeking direction from God without willingly accepting His guidance. When taking problems to God, are you humble and brave enough to obey His counsel? Only then is there sufficient power to conquer any obstacle.

Faith has certain conditions: First, a person cannot doubt. Doubt is having indecision about God's ability to answer a petition.

Secondly, a person must believe: "Without faith it is impossible to please him, for whoever would draw near to God must believe that he exists and that he rewards those who seek him." (Hebrews 11:6)

Expectation

When receiving medical care from a physician, expectation has an important role. The patient who is confident in the prescribed remedy has a greater likelihood of recovery than the one who is uncertain the doctor can provide a cure. In the same way, an answer from God necessitates praying and expecting.

Prayer is more than a mindless ritual or mere formality. The promise of an answer is virtually unqualified, except for belief. Do you pray believing God will answer? Ask and believe that you will receive.

Walking under a ladder is commonly thought to be bad luck. Suppose you come upon a building under construction with a ladder leaning against the wall. Do you walk under the ladder or do you attempt to find a way around it?

Followers of Jesus believe in divine providence and do not view life as a game of chance, involving good and bad luck. Christ and chance run opposite, not parallel. People either believe in Christ or take a chance.

So, as a child of God, would you still avoid walking under a ladder? Probably! Why? Not because you believe an old superstition, but just in case you are wrong. Some people approach prayer not expecting an answer but pray just in case they are wrong. Anticipate answers for whatever you ask from God.

Forgiveness

Effectively praying requires forgiveness. Many

prayers remain unanswered because of bitterness. When hate rules the heart, a barrier has been constructed. Prayer cannot exit walls of resentment.

Speaking to God requires having something in common—a mutual bond. Scripture reveals God is Love. Only with a *heart of love* can a person effectively speak to the *God of ultimate Love*. Love responds to love.

Have you seen the film, "Forrest Gump?" The woman Forrest loved was a reckless teenager of the 60's, sowing wild oats. She is portrayed as drug-addicted and suicidal, eventually dying from AIDS.

What caused her inner turmoil? In one scene, Forrest watches as she throws rocks at her weather-beaten childhood home—a house holding memories of abuse at the hands of her father. When she finally stops throwing stones and begins to weep, Forrest says, "Sometimes, there just aren't enough rocks."

You will never get rid of bitterness by throwing rocks of resentment, rocks of anger, rocks of slander, or rocks of scorn—there just are not enough rocks. Let the Lord tap open any festering wounds filled with bitterness and wash away all the poison by grace. Get rid of contaminating guile!

ACTION

Corrie ten Boom, who hid Jews from the Nazis during WWII, was known for asking, "Is prayer your steering wheel or your spare tire?" Prayer is meant to guide your life, not just fix your problems. Life-directing prayer involves faith, expectation, and forgiveness.

It is not the arithmetic of prayer (how many), or the rhetoric of prayer (how eloquent), or the geometry of prayer (how long), or the music of prayer (how sweet), or the logic of prayer (how argumentative), or the method of prayer (how orderly), that matters. Do you pray persistently believing? Do you pray tirelessly anticipating? Do you pray continuously pardoning?

Communicate to God regularly with mountain-moving prayers!

CHAPTER FIFTEEN

ACCUSED

And as he was walking in the temple, the chief priests and the scribes and the elders came to him.... And he began to speak to them in parables.... And they were seeking to arrest him but feared the people, for they perceived that he had told the parable against them. So they left him and went away. And they sent to him some of the Pharisees and some of the Herodians, to trap him in his talk.... And Sadducees came to him, who say that there is no resurrection. And they asked him a question.... And one of the scribes came up and heard them disputing with one another, and seeing that he answered them well, asked him.... And after that no one dared to ask him any more questions.... "And when they bring you to trial and deliver you over, do not be anxious beforehand what you are to say, but say whatever is given you in that hour, for it is not you who speak, but the Holy Spirit." (Mark 11:37; 12:1, 12-13, 18, 28, 34; 13:11)

It would be nice if people always thought the best of others, but pride, envy, and jealousy make this impossible. As part of the fallen human race, people look for faults more than virtue. Right now, there is a strong probability someone you know is looking for the crack in your armor; is probing for vulnerabilities; is searching for imperfections; is hoping you fail. Wanting the playing field of life to be equal, some are tearing down instead of rising up.

Throughout your life accusers will pass blame or bring unfounded charges. Accusations start as a child (tattling), increase as a teenager (blathering), and intensify as an adult (slandering). No one escapes this tragedy, and everyone needs rescuing.

My family and I arrived at a new ministry assignment only to discover the church was doctrinally divided. A few members quickly became dissatisfied with my teaching and immediately left, one being the treasurer. With financial records in hand, he and his wife came to my office. They were not satisfied with simply turning over the various accounts but wanted the pleasure of blaming me for their departure. After announcing their plans and making a few senseless accusations, they sat waiting for a response.

ACTION

I thanked them for coming and telling me of their decision. I expressed appreciation for their service to the church. I finished by saying their actions would not be considered personal. My family and I had only been in town a few weeks and little time was given to getting acquainted. Their leaving was based on assumptions more than facts. The reply was not well received.

What followed the next several months was a barrage of accusations about me and the church. My wife was not spared from hurtful comments. Rumors abounded about Scriptural truths being neglected and of me not believing in a literal devil. Not only did I believe in the devil but I kept running into a few of his closer friends.

One person claimed the church would be closed in two months. This was personally comforting for the Lord of the church was then obligated to prove the prediction wrong. The congregation weathered the storm but not without pain. They eventually saw better numerical and financial growth, and the struggle brought a greater sense of the Lord's presence.

No matter how honorable your intentions, how pure your motives, and how sincere your convictions, some will be suspicious of you and others will not like you. You can worry, fold, and crumble, or gain sufficiency in the Lord and excel.

Jesus was confronted by people wanting to find fault. When you are the brunt of false accusations, His circumstances serve as a guide.

Know your audience

Four different kinds of accusers questioned Jesus. They represent the main sources of accusations. Each should be treated differently.

When dealing with *chief priests and elders*, Jesus focused on attitude and motives. They were prejudiced and biased, desiring to chastise Him.

Jesus tells a story, giving attention to their heart condition: A landowner entrusts some property to a few competent managers. They started abusing the messengers and eventually took the life of his son, proving to be untrustworthy. Terrible consequences soon followed.

Although blinded by bigotry, they quickly understood the story was about them. Shamed and humiliated, they sought revenge. The most dangerous kind of accuser looks at life through prejudicial eyes.

When dealing with *Pharisees and Herodians*, Jesus uses common sense. They were highly intelligent and political, desiring to entrap Him. They attempted to ensnare by debating the issue of faith in God and civic responsibility; the dispute over separation of religion and government is not new.

Jesus challenges the logic and foundation of their argument. A commonly held value among socially elite and influential politicians is popularity and money, constantly worrying if the economy will keep them in office and if there is ample revenue to gain favors and votes? Instead of quoting Scripture, He uses their monetary value system to dispel the case.

When dealing with *Sadducees*, Jesus focuses on the interpretation of Scripture. They were religious and judgmental, desiring to stupefy Jesus and make Him appear foolish. Their challenge came in the form of a hypothetical question—the age-old attempt to discount truth through absurdity.

Jesus exposes their tunnel vision, saying, "You fail to comprehend the fullness of Scripture that you preciously embrace and adhere to." The Bible is either interpreted literally, literalistically, or figuratively. How Scripture is construed determines belief. Jesus challenges their faulty approach to divine truth.

When dealing with *Scribes*, Jesus quotes sacred verses. They were arrogant educators, desiring to belittle Jesus. He let Scripture speak for itself.

Genuine scholars recognize the truth, cherish truth, and never violate truth.

They asked Jesus about the most important fact of life, requiring a two-part answer: First, God is one; idols and the devil are not gods. Secondly, true wisdom is based on intimacy, not insight. Intelligent people love the Lord rather than simply know about Him. The academicians left amazed.

These accusers will be yours, as well. Know your audience! Reciting Bible verses does not work with people failing to base life upon Scripture. Debating Scriptural truths is useless with people interpreting divine writings differently. Who is making accusations? Respond accordingly!

Answer the question

Some people answer questions by sidestepping the issue.

An older college professor taught New Testament survey. Year after year, the course grade was determined solely by the results of the final exam, which was always the same essay question: "Describe and analyze the journeys of the Apostle Paul."

Word got out among the students that the course was an easy "A", simply prepare for the final essay question. The class became a favorite for football players, not typically known for possessing brainpower.

One year, the professor changed the question: "Examine and critique the teachings of Jesus in the Sermon on the Mount." The football players were mortified, they sat without writing a word. The dumbest player on the team, however, was feverishly writing until time ran out.

The grades were posted and every team member failed, except the dumbest player who got a "D". The team could not believe it and asked how he knew anything about the Sermon on the Mount. He said, "I just replied, 'Who am I to criticize the words of the Master, but let me tell you about the journeys of the Apostle Paul.'" Do you sidestep or answer the question?

Other people reply with too much information.

I am fascinated at what my mother-in-law can do to a simple question. I grew up in a home where responses were direct and brief. If asked something as simple as, "Where were you?" a typical reply could be, "I went to the store to buy bread."

My mother-in-law, a wonderful and godly woman, would respond like this: "I was going to the store (I think something is wrong with the car, it seems to be acting up). When I got into the parking lot another driver almost hit me; I took down the plate number and plan to call the police. I saw Martha entering the store; do you know she is getting married next month? While going toward the bread aisle I saw the nicest display of dishes and wondered if you needed any? After picking the freshest loaf of bread, I noticed donuts on sale and got a dozen. The check-out clerk told me that next week's ad has lots of great buys." She can make a novel out of a short story.

Many people are not much different, saying too much and eventually having statements used against them. When answering more than asked, the simplicity of truth easily becomes lost. Give accurate answers without saying too much.

Reveal Jesus

Accusers often struggle with a *position* more than a *person*. Jesus spoke of having a special position with God. Some accusing Him may have personally liked Him, but were troubled by His unique heavenly status. He did not take personal offense, recognizing struggles are against principalities and powers, not flesh and blood. All conflicts are primarily spiritual in nature.

Rely on the Holy Spirit, and Jesus will be seen in your conversations. He instructs followers, "It is not you speaking but the Holy Spirit." (13:11) The Spirit has come to remind you of Jesus—teaching and guiding you in His ways.

The use of alcoholic beverages can be a hot-button among believers. The primary debate is justifying the use of mind-altering drinks that have ruined and enslaved countless lives.

One argument, used in favor of alcoholic consumption, comes from the book of Proverbs, stating drunkenness and gluttony are equally wrong. Since church people constantly eat too much without chastisement, why frown upon intoxicating beverages?

A young couple was using this line of reasoning with me. The wife said, "I don't see any difference between overeating and an occasional drink!" sadly comparing over-indulgence with moderation. Sensing an out-of-ordinary divine prompting, I responded, "The difference is that wives are not usually beaten by overeating husbands but are often beaten by intoxicated ones. The difference is the outcome."

When grace is challenged, the Holy Spirit helps you respond.

ACTION

If confronted by accusers, approach your audience differently: are they prejudice, influential, judgmental, or scholarly? Answer only the question. And reveal Jesus!

One final unpleasant thought: No matter what you say or do, you may still end up crucified.

If it happened to Jesus, it can happen to you—if they did it to Jesus, they may do it to you.

CHAPTER SIXTEEN

LOOSE ENDS

And as [Jesus] sat on the Mount of Olives opposite the temple, Peter and James and John and Andrew asked him privately, "Tell us, when will these things be, and what will be the sign when all these things are about to be accomplished?" (Mark 13:3-4)

The Olivet Discourse is sometimes called, "The Little Apocalypse", briefly dealing with events surrounding end times. The conversation occurred only a few days before the crucifixion.

Think about your activities when preparing for a long trip: suspending newspaper and mail delivery; servicing the vehicle; arranging for pet care; organizing clothes; packing; ensuring appliances are turned off; verifying windows and doors are locked; loading vehicle; re-loading vehicle; loading vehicle a third and final time; briefly praying before leaving the driveway; returning for a forgotten item; leaving again with a vow to buy whatever else is needed. My home has gone through these routines numerous times.

Jesus was soon departing. What was He thinking? Could He have been wondering: "Is the training complete? Are the instructions sufficient? Is the Kingdom of God understandable? What requires additional emphasis? What needs reminding?"

When our children grew older, leaving the house and starting careers, my wife and I had similar questions: "Did we do right? Did we give good tools for success? Did we do too much, crippling them of achievement? Will they accomplish their dreams? Will they end up fulfilled?"

Some unfinished business needed further emphasis before going to the cross of Golgotha. Jesus gave attention to loose ends—the final exclamation point to His training.

Correction: Church is not a facility!

While walking by the temple, a disciple said, "Look at the beautiful stones and stately structure!" Jesus replied, "See the great Temple? Not one stone will be left upon another; they will be thrown down." (Mark 13:1-2)

Herod's temple was one of the most beautiful buildings in the Near East. The historian Josephus wrote about majestic white marble pillars and walkways paved with mosaic stones. Brass doors were decorated with precious metals and every wall was richly ornamented with gold, inside and out. The furnishings included gold utensils embedded with jewels, and curtains made of the finest and richest material. The place was impressive and magnificent, its elegance commanded attention.

Regardless the splendor, the structure was completely destroyed, the heavy stones cast over the wall. The prophetical pronouncement made by Jesus was fulfilled some 40 years later.

Tragically, many placing hope in a *location* more than the *Lord*, look for God in a *place* instead of a *Person*, and experience grief. Some even lose faith. Jesus said, "I will build my church, and the gates of hell shall not prevail against it." (Matthew 16:18) God's kingdom is not an institution, easily destroyed by hateful people or evil leaders. If laws forbid places of worship, His kingdom continues. His realm resides in believers, gathering triumphantly everywhere.

The church is not an ark for saving a select few; a pleasure ship experiencing a pleasant voyage; a ferryboat taking effortless passengers to the shores of heaven; a life insurance company, only obligating policyholders with a small annual premium; a social guild welcoming certain people and excluding others.

The church is a lifeboat rescuing weary and broken lives; a union for loving everybody; a family in which love and service is expected from one another; a community providing constant opportunities for ongoing growth and development; a company of believers personally discovering the one way of life and obeying the one Lord of life; a center of worship where people collectively come to God for encouragement.

The church is the representative of Jesus on earth, reflecting His nature and governed by His will. Look for God in people, transformed by resurrection power, rather than in artistically designed facilities.

Instruction: Tell everyone the Good News!

The gospel must be proclaimed to all nations. (Mark 13:10) The assignment is not complete until the whole world hears His story.

The magnitude of the opportunity is overwhelming, yet possible. James Kennedy, the founder of Evangelism Explosion, made this observation: When Peter preached his first sermon, over 3000 believed. Shortly thereafter, 5000 were added, followed by a great multitude of Jews and priests! Next came a period of persecution. When it ended in AD 313 with the Edict of Toleration, ten million professing Christians were alive. By the year 1000, the number had grown to fifty million. By the end of the 1700's, the missionary impetus had stalled, yet the number was 215 million professing Christians—an increase of 169 million in eight hundred years.

In 1795, the modern missionary movement began in earnest with William Carey. By the year 1900, the number had grown to five hundred million—an increase of 285 million in one century. By 1980, just eighty years later, the number had grown to 1.3 billion. By 1990, the number was roughly 1.8 billion—an increase of 1.3 billion people in the 20th century alone.

David Barrett, a church demographer, compared the estimated number of committed believers with the number of non-believing people in the world at different points in time: By 1430, 1 out of 99 followed Jesus; by 1790, 1 out of 49; by 1960, 1 out of 24; by 1980, 1 out of 16; by 1983, 1 out of 13; by 1986, 1 out of 11; by 1989, 1 out of 10; by 1993, 1 out of 9 followed Jesus.

The church is demonstrating a divinely anointed ambition to finish the task. Every believer must tell

His story until all have heard.

Warning: Falsehood will increase!

Deception will multiply near the end of time. Most errors will come beautifully packaged and hard to detect. False anointed ones and prophets will arise, performing signs and wonders and, if possible, leading believers astray. Jesus wants His followers on guard! (Mark 13:22-23)

E. Stanley Jones commented, "Each system must be judged by its output, its fruit. The outcome is the criterion. What are we trying to produce? The ends of the different systems of thought and faith may be summed up as follows: Greece said be moderate and be yourself; Rome said be strong and order yourself; Confucianism says be superior and correct yourself; Shintoism says be loyal and suppress yourself; Buddhism says be disillusioned and annihilate yourself; Hinduism says be separated and merge yourself; Mohammedanism says be submissive and assert yourself; Judaism says be holy and conform yourself; Modern materialism says be industrious and enjoy yourself; Modern Dilettantism says be broad and cultivate yourself; Christianity says be Christlike and give yourself."

One of the greatest dangers people face today is materialism. Worldwide economic systems are built on acquiring large quantities of possessions.

Good people are dying fulfilling the American dream and spending eternity separated from God. Many humane, kind, generous, and caring people have yet to place faith in God and may one day hear Jesus say the tragic words, "Sorry, I never knew you."

Following Jesus is the only pathway to complete freedom, to a relationship with God, and to an eternal home. You cannot earn everlasting life with *stuff*.

Comfort: Expect Jesus to return!

Jesus said, "When you see these things taking place, you know that he is near, at the very gates. Truly, I say to you, this generation will not pass away until all these things take place. Heaven and earth will pass away, but my words will not pass away." (Mark 13:29-31)

Circumstances throughout the world occasionally appear bleak, but cannot last forever. A day is quickly coming when God will say, "The end!"

A shout will be heard around the world, waking the dead in Christ. The trumpet of heaven will sound, summoning His people to a caught up experience. The church will be gathered and united with the Lord for eternity.

Skeptics have, and always will, scoff. They will downplay the seriousness of conditions and desensitize society of any concern. They will sneer and make light of the situation, *but only until it happens*. God will deal with finality the results of sin and evil. The consequences will be greater than anything ever before witnessed on earth.

Those following Jesus are to take comfort in their full and complete salvation. The struggles of life will soon be over, and the afflictions of life cannot enter *time without end*. Keep looking for His return; it is closer than many expect.

ACTION

Jesus took care of these loose ends before His crucifixion: words of correction, instruction, warning, and comfort. As some of the last private statements made to His disciples, they held special significance. If the Twelve acted on these words, they would see Him again, as well as countless others. They did act!

It is now up to you to keep acting on these particulars: God resides in people; tell His story to everyone; watch out for falsehood; look for His soon coming. *Maranatha*!

CHAPTER SEVENTEEN

DYING

And they went to a place called Gethsemane. And he said to his disciples, "Sit here while I pray." And he took with him Peter and James and John, and began to be greatly distressed and troubled. And he said to them, "My soul is very sorrowful, even to death. Remain here and watch." And going a little farther, he fell on the ground and prayed that, if it were possible, the hour might pass from him. And he said, "Abba, Father, all things are possible for you. Remove this cup from me. Yet not what I will, but what you will." (Mark 14:32-36)

The Mount of Olives is the last private *conversation* Jesus had with the Twelve, giving attention to end times and His second coming. Gethsemane is the last private *moment* Jesus had with His friends, teaching another great lesson.

As a young college student, I took it upon myself to read the first eight chapters of Mark in one sitting. Jesus suddenly became flesh and blood to me. He seemed very human while completely Divine. His experiences ministered to many of my needs and shortcomings.

Excited by what happened, I read the last eight chapters the following day. I was stunned by what occurred next. A deep, dark hidden fear surfaced from my soul, and victory came to an issue troubling me since early childhood.

What caused such anxiety? I had a tremendous fear of dying.

As a little boy, I woke up many times in the middle of the night gripped by fears of death. One time, I ran upstairs to my mother, buried my face in her lap, and sobbingly cried, "I don't want to die!" She hugged me and stroked my hair for the longest time saying, "What are you worried about? You're just a little boy." She tried her best to comfort but I knew death sometimes happens to little boys.

A classmate died at age sixteen. He was an upcoming star in the Seattle music industry, a sax player and leader of a rock band. On the way to a performance, he died in a vehicle collision. High School students deeply mourned his death and confronted their mortality.

ACTION

My best friend was killed in Vietnam. We were as close as the Biblical friendship of David and Jonathan. I struggled for years accepting his untimely death. My eyes still water when viewing his name on the Vietnam Memorial Wall.

What was Jesus saying when He declared, "My soul is deeply grieved?" Why did He groan, "If possible, let this hour pass by me?"

He would soon experience severe agony: the sinless Savior would be stained by sickening sin; the beloved Son of God would sense rejection from the Heavenly Father. Intertwined with inward anguish was outward apprehension. Jesus wanted to avoid the universal consequence of sin.

The Garden of Gethsemane shows a man hoping not to go through the final experience of life, yet finding sufficiency by praying.

Matthew writes to religious Jews, Luke writes to thinking Greeks, and Mark writes to industrious Romans, many of them facing martyrdom and needing courage. The story of Jesus addresses challenges and difficulties caused by living in a hostile environment. Mark shows Jesus facing human struggles and limitations, identifying with life and death. What is more important: Faith to live, or faith to die?

The certainty

Everyone lives under the shadow of mortality. Young couples often avoid discussing funeral arrangements, acting as if talking about death causes it to happen. The subject may not fit honeymoon plans but needs attention early in a marriage. Dying is a natural part of living.

Death came because of human rebellion. Is God cruel for issuing such harsh punishment? On the contrary, He lovingly decided to not allow people to live in sinfulness forever. Living in eternal wickedness would be endless despair. He pronounced death and made provision for a liberated eternity. As long as sin exists, there needs to be death.

A teaching went through the church that people of faith did not have to experience death, based on the life of Enoch and Elijah. Enoch walked with God and was taken. (Genesis 5:24) Elijah experienced a heavenward chariot ride. (2 Kings 2:11) The belief promoted that faith could translate people into heaven.

Until caught up at His return, followers of Jesus have an appointment with death. (Hebrews 9:27) Everyone dies!

The only known kind of living includes dying.

People make choices every day illumined by the possibility of death. My dad feared heights and asked me to paint the high points of the house. A friend feared motorcycles, calling them "skull crushers" to discourage his children from riding them.

As a teenager, I water skied but never desired to snow ski; too many friends came back from the slopes with broken legs, one came home paralyzed. Unlike the television slogan, I never saw the thrill of victory, only the agony of defeat.

An old saying is very true: "The only thing you have to do in life is die!"

The experience

Living is a normal aspiration. Humans were initially created without death. When the experience seems imminent, the natural action is to resist and fight. Desiring to die is not normal. If someone pursues death, something has gone emotionally wrong.

People become fascinated with near death stories, usually referring to walking toward a bright light and feeling serenity. Although God is Light and Love, Scripture does not substantiate these actions and sensations occurring at the time of death.

The clearest Biblical understanding of dying is

falling asleep. The Apostle Paul wrote, "We do not want you to be uninformed, brothers, about those who are asleep, that you may not grieve as others do who have no hope. (1 Thessalonians 4:13)

Sleep involves a person moving from awake to slumber and, after a seemingly brief period, back to consciousness. The experience of dying is like falling asleep to this world and immediately waking up in heavenly rest. The dying process is practiced every time you lay down at the end of the day.

"We are always of good courage. We know that while we are at home in the body we are away from the Lord." (2 Corinthians 5:6) A day is coming when the opposite will be true—away from the body and home with the Lord.

Dying is like a tunnel. In the Black Hills of South Dakota, near Mount Rushmore, is Iron Mountain Road—a winding highway with single-lane tunnels. Peering through one of them, you can clearly see in the distance the faces of Washington, Jefferson, Roosevelt, and Lincoln. Similarly, death is only a glimpse of what is ahead—a division point between two halves of living. Presently, life is *partially* seen but someday will be *fully* known (1 Corinthians 13:12), the tunnel of death being the dividing point.

Everyone hopes for a pain-free moment,

preferably while asleep in bed. No one knows the means of their departure, but following Jesus gives sufficient grace to see a person home.

The blessing

Can death be a blessing? Paul wrote, "…to live is Christ and to die is gain…. I am hard pressed between the two. My desire is to depart and be with Christ, for that is far better. But to remain in the flesh is more necessary on your account." (Philippians 1:21, 23-24)

The Northern Kingdom of Israel was initially ruled by Solomon's servant, Jeroboam. He taught the nation to sin, leading them into wicked idolatry. His son became ill and the king sent his wife to a prophet, disguised as another woman. The rouse was divinely exposed, and judgment was rendered.

The consequences included, "Anyone belonging to Jeroboam who dies in the city the dogs shall eat, and anyone who dies in the open country the birds of the heavens shall eat, for the LORD has spoken it. Arise therefore, go to your house. When your feet enter the city, the child shall die. And all Israel shall mourn for him and bury him, for he only of Jeroboam shall come to the grave, because in him there is found something pleasing to the LORD, the God of Israel, in the house of Jeroboam." (1 Kings 14:11-13) The child was spared from his father's punishment. Death can be kindhearted instead of cruel.

I knew a man dying from cancer. The last two years of his life were physically exhausting. The disease caused great discomfort. He struggled gasping for every breath. I occasionally visited him at a Veterans Hospital to read Scripture and pray, something he greatly appreciated.

At the funeral home, his weary body finally looked restful. However, his peaceful countenance was not the source of comfort for his wife. Knowing he was whole again gave her greater peace.

Life has so much tragedy that death sometimes comes as healing. For those following Jesus, wholeness follows death: no more discomfort and pain; no blindness, lameness, deafness, or disease. Dying is a one time experience, victoriously consumed in Christ. The sting is gone! (1 Corinthians 15)

ACTION

People decide to follow Jesus for mainly one of two reasons: seeking purpose or fearing death. I happened to be afraid of dying. Basing such an important decision on the inevitable is not wrong. If the second coming of the Lord does not occur in your lifetime, you will journey into eternity through death's door.

For those following Jesus, there is nothing cruel about death. When believers die, they go to a specially prepared place, beautifully designed. "Precious in the sight of the LORD is the death of his saints." (Psalms 116:15)

Jesus demonstrated a *faith to live by* in the region of Galilee, and a *faith to die by* in the garden of Gethsemane. Not only have faith to live, but also to die.

I said, "I don't want to die." Neither did Jesus! He gained victory in a garden of prayer. You can do the same.

CHAPTER EIGHTEEN
DENYING

Jesus said to him, "Truly, I tell you, this very night, before the rooster crows twice, you will deny me three times." But [Peter] said emphatically, "If I must die with you, I will not deny you." ... And he came and found them sleeping, and he said to Peter, "Simon, are you asleep? Could you not watch one hour? Watch and pray that you may not enter into temptation." ... Peter had followed him at a distance, right into the courtyard of the high priest. And he was sitting with the guards and warming himself at the fire.... As Peter was below in the courtyard, one of the servant girls of the high priest came, and seeing Peter warming himself, she looked at him and said, "You also were with the Nazarene, Jesus." But he denied it, saying, "I neither know nor understand what you mean." And he went out into the gateway and the rooster crowed. And the servant girl saw him and began again to say to the bystanders, "This man is one of them." But again he denied it. And after a little while the bystanders again said to Peter, "Certainly you are one of them, for you are a Galilean." But he began to invoke a curse on himself and to swear, "I do not know this man of whom you speak." And immediately the rooster crowed a second time. ... The Lord turned and looked at Peter. And Peter remembered the saying of the Lord, how he said to Him, "Before the rooster crows today, you will deny me three times." And he went out and wept bitterly. ... "But go, tell his disciples and Peter.... (Mark 14:30-31,37-38,54,66-72; Luke 22:61-62; Mark 16:7)

When angrily confronted about your relationship with God, two options exist: dying or denying. Mark addressed the topic of *dying* in a garden and of *denying* in a courtyard, both on the same night.

Denial means failing to acknowledge, or disavowing a friendship. Has someone refused to vouch for you at a critical moment? If a personal reference about your integrity and abilities is not positive, expect to feel anguish.

An experience just as terrible as being denied is denying. If associating with someone could possibly damage your relationship with others, jeopardize your career, or trigger harassment and tribulation, would you disavow knowing them?

Jesus experienced the pain of *rejection*, and Peter felt the emptiness of *rejecting*. How could this have happened? He witnessed Jesus performing numerous miracles and multiple healings; he had the special privilege of seeing Jesus transformed on the Mount of Transfiguration; he followed Jesus daily with boldness and enthusiasm. Even during their final meal, he told Jesus he would be numbered with the dying, but ended up listed with the denying.

Luke gives an additional piece of information about the incident: Jesus turned and gazed at Peter—not a look of surprise, but an invitation to remember. Reminded of his pledge to die, how did Peter feel being confronted with the act of denying? Despair must have sucked abundant life right out of him! He lost a friend—Mentor, Master, Messiah—and fled weeping.

What about you? Are you denying the Lord? Could the source of an uneasy feeling be Jesus staring at your soul? In what ways can He be denied?

Failing to live His life before others

Does your lifestyle clearly reveal a close friendship with God? When was the last time you told someone about your faith in Christ?

Did the young maiden in the courtyard wonder: "Peter, why are you sitting idly by while we condemn your Teacher? Why is nothing being said or done? Your passivity exonerates those making sport of your Friend!"

People constantly examine actions and quickly recognize the commitment level of His followers. Denial occurs by refusing to represent Jesus before family, friends, neighbors, classmates, or business associates.

Ask yourself tough questions: Am I remaining silent when others make fun of faith or slander God? Am I conforming to the ways of non-believers instead of living a life reflective of Him?

Jesus said, "Whoever denies me before men, I also will deny before my Father who is in heaven." (Matthew 10:33)

Faith in God naturally exposes the spiritual rebellion in others. "For at one time you were darkness, but now you are light in the Lord. Walk as children of light (for the fruit of light is found in all that is good and right and true) and try to discern what is pleasing to the Lord. Take no part in the unfruitful works of darkness, but instead expose them." (Ephesians 5:8-11)

Unfortunately, some who reference the Church, the Bible, and the Lord, laugh at crude humor and participate in foolish behavior, initiated by people residing in spiritual darkness. Live His life and bring light to the darkness in others.

Knowing His will and failing to do it

Jesus said, "Everyone who hears these words of mine and does not do them will be like a foolish man who built his house on the sand. And the rain fell, and the floods came, and the winds blew and beat against that house, and it fell, and great was the fall of it." (Matthew 7:26-27)

Failing to use gifts and talents for Jesus, and failing to actively perform acts of service, is denying His Lordship over your life. The Old Testament prophet Jonah was a man with a calling who decided to disobey. He ran headlong into trouble and positioned himself for greater frustration and bitterness. Resentment and discontent are often linked to refusing to render humble service to the Lord.

Has the Holy Spirit been tugging at your heart about helping? Are you digging in your heels and stubbornly refusing to serve or give support to God's work? Spare yourself the sorrow of Peter who failed the Lord in an hour of need, spare yourself personal disappointment and distress. *Remember*: talents and resources are to be invested in Christ.

Dethroning the Lord

Peter did not comprehend why Jesus was going through an unjust trial and facing a cruel death. He did not grasp His suffering was linked to an eternal solution. Faith involves not fully understanding His plans or how they become implemented.

When confronted with inexplicable tragedy, do you dethrone the Lord? If family members die an untimely death, or friends get critically injured, do you reject God?

Some make faulty conclusions about the Lord: He must not care, or is not powerful. Questioning is not wrong but denying the love and might of the Savior is a mistake. Some answers await your arrival in eternity.

God works in every situation, whether you understand it or not. The steps of the righteous are ordered by Him and He is greater than any difficulty. He brings you through unpleasant circumstances and makes them advantageous. He is never uncaring or too weak and always works to your benefit.

Avoid the temptation of denying His greatness because of everyday occurrences.

ACTION

Positioning yourself to deny

At no time did Peter plan to renounce his association with Jesus, yet he journeyed to Gethsemane tired and grew weary keeping watch. Denial occurs when believers are careless about praying. Being full of good intentions but inactive in prayer is a recipe for failure.

"Therefore, let anyone who thinks that he stands take heed lest he fall." (1 Corinthians 10:12)

No one is invincible. Denying can happen to anyone, even bold and daring followers of Jesus. When feeling physically and emotionally drained, praying needs to intensify.

Denial also occurs in places where the act is virtually inevitable. What was Peter doing at the High Priest's house? No one can hang out with unsavory characters without eventually being challenged about their relationship with God. Believers do not belong in some environments.

Unfortunately, people knowing God go casually to inappropriate places, into environments of abuse and deception. Sadly, they choose to go and are rarely forced. Why? For the same reason Peter was in the courtyard—to observe a spectacle. Disgusting surroundings challenge an allegiance with God.

What can be done after denying?

First, repent! Peter wept bitter tears. Repentance is more than just saying, "I'm sorry." Repentance means yielding your life to His Lordship once again. The look causing Peter to search his soul is the same one beckoning everyone to change directions and transform actions. With repentance comes forgiveness and cleansing.

Secondly, accept forgiveness! The rest of Peter's story is recorded in Mark 16, 'Tell his disciples *and Peter*...." (V. 7) Peter had distanced himself from the other disciples and was summoned to rejoin them.

God forgives, but people are often unwilling to forgive themselves. Some even seek comfort through personal condemnation rather than divine grace. If feeling a sense of shame, avoid separating yourself from the church. Detaching from other believers only gives further opportunity for the devil. Both repentance and acceptance are required.

ACTION

Denial is an ugly word, but not a fatal or final word. Mark's recording of His story is most likely *Peter's personal reflections*. He discovered there is grace upon grace found in Christ. That same grace is available to all those who do not want to die and have no plans to deny.

CHAPTER NINETEEN

THE CROSS

They crucified him and divided his garments among them, casting lots for them, to decide what each should take. And it was the third hour when they crucified him. And the inscription of the charge against him read, "The King of the Jews." And with him they crucified two robbers, one on his right and one on his left. And those who passed by derided him, wagging their heads and saying, "Aha! You who would destroy the temple and rebuild it in three days, save yourself, and come down from the cross!" So also the chief priests with the scribes mocked him to one another, saying, "He saved others; he cannot save himself. Let the Christ, the King of Israel, come down now from the cross that we may see and believe." Those who were crucified with him also reviled him. (Mark 15:24-32)

If it happened to Jesus, it can happen to you—if they did it to Jesus, they may do it to you.

This part of Jesus life is not enjoyable reading, yet is the primary reason for His story being told. He was viciously attacked in two arenas: one religious and the other political. Unfortunately, the political only got involved after being egged on by the religious. Sanctimonious priests manipulated a government official to achieve an unjust end. These two systems, designed for domination, often make strange bedfellows, producing foul odors.

His torturous death says something significant about salvation and spiritual formation. Philippians connects the dots: "Indeed, I count everything as loss because of the surpassing worth of knowing Christ Jesus my Lord. For his sake I have suffered the loss of all things and count them as rubbish, in order that I may gain Christ and be found in him, not having a righteousness of my own that comes from the law, but that which comes through faith in Christ, the righteousness from God that depends on faith—that I may know him and the power of his resurrection, and may share his sufferings, becoming like him in his death, that by any means possible I may attain the resurrection from the dead." (Philippians 3:8-11) *His crucifixion reveals your cross.*

One of the great ironies of life is how worldly

corruption aids spiritual development. Dishonesty and deception, coming from others, trigger an agony that completes new life in you.

When deplorable actions are dished out, followers of Jesus are kept dependent on the resurrected Lord. Through painful trials, supernatural grace is experienced. The more you are made conformable to the death of Jesus, the more you will share *daily* in resurrection power.

Most followers want to avoid the cross but cannot. If you want the power of resurrection, if you want His glory manifested in great and tremendous ways, then you must not only identify with His suffering but become fashioned to His death.

When someone hangs on a cross, they are not going anyplace unless someone carries them. When someone hangs on a cross, they have no future plans as it pertains to this world—no ambitions or desires. When someone hangs on a cross, they are not holding on to anything, they have turned loose of everything.

The message of Golgotha is *die out to self and enter a new life*. Unjust harassment forces the examination of sincerity, character, and the fitness of the soul. The cruelty of others assists transformation. No one is expected to enjoy the dreadful process.

Submission

"The chief priests accused him of many things. And Pilate again asked him, 'Have you no answer to make? See how many charges they bring against you.' But Jesus made no further answer, so that Pilate was amazed." (Mark 15:3-5)

The charges were bogus, many accusations being on the far side of ridiculous. Envious leaders distorted the truth about Jesus and His message. Even Pilate recognized their jealousy. (V. 10) Yet Jesus remained silent, submitting His life to His accusers and refusing to respond in His own defense. The Lion of Judah could have leaped and devoured, but the Lamb of God made an appearance.

Have your actions ever been misinterpreted? Has there ever been a time when saying anything would only make matters worse? Have you ever gone through a situation in which the best thing you could do was remain silent? Then you can identify with Jesus and, better yet, He identifies with you.

You may have wanted to defend yourself, but divine power is not manifested when matters are taken into your own hands. When forced into silent submission, resurrection power is experienced.

Shame

"And the soldiers led him away inside the palace (that is, the governor's headquarters), and they called together the whole battalion. And they clothed him in a purple cloak, and twisting together a crown of thorns, they put it on him. And they began to salute him, 'Hail, King of the Jews!' And they were striking his head with a reed and spitting on him and kneeling down in homage to him. And when they had mocked him, they stripped him of the purple cloak and put his own clothes on him. And they led him out to crucify him." (Mark 15:16-20)

Tormentors made sport of Jesus. They stupidly perceived Him a clown, not the Christ. He became a joke and His message was scorned. They attempted to suppress the truth by shaming Him.

Many attempt the same today by mocking the faith and personal beliefs of His followers. Some foolishly determine truth from error and right from wrong using manipulation and coercion, thinking domination proves rightness.

What does shame actually damage in a believer? Humiliation only gives unwholesome pride a beating. Believers mistakenly react to shame with malice, but a fatally wounded pride leads to new life. Disgrace aids your efforts to be humble, manifesting the power that raised Jesus from the dead.

Sacrifice

"Those who passed by derided him, wagging their heads and saying, 'Aha! You who would destroy the temple and rebuild it in three days, save yourself, and come down from the cross!' So also the chief priests with the scribes mocked him to one another, saying, 'He saved others; he cannot save himself. Let the Christ, the King of Israel, come down now from the cross that we may see and believe.' Those who were crucified with him also reviled him." (Mark 15:29-32)

While experiencing excruciating physical torture, citizens, clergy, and criminals were deriding, mocking, and reviling Jesus. Already submissive and shamed, the crowd was now adding insult to injury.

What was He thinking while this commotion was taking place? Did He wonder, "Why am I sacrificing my life for them?" Jesus could have said, "Enough!" and called myriads of angels to His rescue.

Have you ever felt like you have sacrificed enough—financially gave enough, served long enough, attended enough times? Unfortunately, some go to the next level and think, "When will it be my turn?" Statements about *enough* and *my turn* are dangerous indicators of misplaced priorities and erroneous thinking.

Jesus never said, "Enough!" rather, "No one takes my life; I lay it down." He decided to willingly sacrifice His life and not condemn people for foolish behavior.

Life consists of choices. Very few things are *taken* from you; very little fits into the category of *unconditional* surrender. You must face daily the war of choices. Decisions are demanded from you—decisions about sacrifice.

What is your decision between God's plan and personal preference? When wants, ambitions, and comforts are *willingly* sacrificed, you position yourself to experience resurrection power.

ACTION

I had several friends and numerous acquaintances growing up. At sixteen, I decided to follow Jesus. Not long afterward, some started saying I was a great guy before I "got religion". They considered me dead, but God graciously gave me new life. Similarly, some may consider you crucified, but God sees you fully alive. His opinion is the only one that matters.

You must put position, prestige, power, and possessions on the cross, recognizing you go nowhere unless the Lord carries you and have nothing unless He provides. The cross is a place without plans, ambitions or desires—a place in which nothing is held on to very tightly as it pertains to this world. You turn loose of everything and identify solely with Jesus. Resurrection is experienced *after* crucifixion.

CHAPTER TWENTY

RELATIONSHIPS

When the Sabbath was past, Mary Magdalene, Mary the mother of James, and Salome bought spices, so that they might go and anoint him. And very early on the first day of the week, when the sun had risen, they went to the tomb. And they were saying to one another, "Who will roll away the stone for us from the entrance of the tomb?" And looking up, they saw that the stone had been rolled back—it was very large. And entering the tomb, they saw a young man sitting on the right side, dressed in a white robe, and they were alarmed. And he said to them, "Do not be alarmed. You seek Jesus of Nazareth, who was crucified. He has risen; he is not here. See the place where they laid him. (Mark 16:1-6)

The end of Mark's writings has an element of controversy. Verse nine and what follows is omitted in some of the older manuscripts. Everything in these verses is expressed elsewhere in Scripture, giving them validation. However, I am limiting my reflections to only the first eight verses. Three thoughts surface—ministry, stone, and barrier.

Ministry

A great joy of my life was becoming acquainted with Harold Carter, pastor of New Shiloh Baptist Church in Baltimore, Maryland—a dynamic Spirit-filled black preacher. I enjoyed our conversations together. I once heard him give a unique description of the church, Christ's special love. He thought Jesus loved seeing His bride in different gowns, such as, the Presbyterian dress, the Methodist dress, the Baptist dress, the Pentecostal dress.

Church affiliations have various beliefs; a few groups are uncomfortable credentialing women for ministry, not allowing ordination. Women have been limited in church work by tradition and culture, some have limited themselves.

A few female followers of Jesus came to the burial site to address a need, to anoint the body of Jesus and make proper preparation for His entombment.

The Bible reveals that women had a significant role in the redemption story. The aged Sarah believed

God, along with Abraham, for a child of promise. A Jericho resident, Rahab, hid Hebrew spies and was spared from destruction, ending up in the ancestry of the Messiah. The devoted foreigner Ruth became the great-grandmother of King David, also included in the genealogy of Jesus. Queen Esther saved the Jewish race from total extinction—a holiday annually celebrated. A virtuous virgin named Mary bore the Son of God.

Luke records that a woman made her home the location for church gatherings in the city of Philippi. (Acts 16:15) Paul's letter to the same church mentions two female workers who "shared his struggle in the cause of the gospel." (Philippians 4:2)

A significant number of Assemblies of God churches in Minnesota were founded by the efforts of women, including the church overseen by me for five years. Four decades later, the founding ladies still attended the church and continued being active in ministry.

A comparison of world religions reveals faith in Jesus has done more to elevate the place of womanhood than any other religion. In Christ, men and women are "joint heirs" of the divine Kingdom. The church is indebted to women in ministry. Much is being accomplished through their love and diligence.

All ministries are equal but not the same. Every act of service is important. Two siblings show the difference: "Six days before the Passover, Jesus therefore came to Bethany, where Lazarus was, whom Jesus had raised from the dead. So, they gave a dinner for him there. Martha served, and Lazarus was one of those reclining with him at table. Mary therefore took a pound of expensive ointment made from pure nard, and anointed the feet of Jesus and wiped his feet with her hair. The house was filled with the fragrance of the perfume." (John 12:1-3)

Who performed better ministry, Martha serving or Mary anointing? Attending to needs with God-given abilities is ministry. Both rendered important service: Martha served Jesus at His table; Mary served Jesus at His feet. They were busy providing heartfelt ministry and giving invaluable service to the Lord.

Differences in personal interests can sometimes cause misunderstanding. Martha accused her sister of not doing her fair share of *table* ministry, but Mary considered *feet* ministry more urgent. (Luke 10) Mary was not more pious, and Martha was not more faithless.

Dorcas was made famous acting like Martha. (Acts 9) Lydia was made famous acting like Mary. (Acts 16)

My mother-in-law is more like Martha. Although she joyfully attended prayer meetings, she really loved the kitchen. Her meals and pies ministered to people. Pastors cherished the goodies she regularly brought to their home.

Some people are more inclined towards visible ministries, while others prefer behind-the-scenes ministries. Both are needed. Regardless of gender, everyone has a ministry.

Be who you are and use your talents for Jesus. The church advances when every believer faithfully serves with all their capabilities.

Stone

A question sometimes surfaces about the empty tomb: Who moved the stone? The most comfortable answer is: God! Was the stone removed to let Jesus out? More likely, to allow the public to look in.

Stones are removed so others can witness the resurrected Lord.

People usually have a good number of unwholesome vises before following Jesus—blockages preventing others from seeing Him. The obstructions are extremely large and not within one's power to take away. Only God can remove obstacles preventing friends and acquaintances from recognizing resurrection power.

Cheating, lying, and stealing are increasingly commonplace today, considered more convenient than honesty and truthfulness. Some believers feel personally obligated to remove these offensive stones and to reform offenders. The greater need is Spirit-empowered transformation.

The best efforts to reform usually fail. Bring them to an encounter with God. The Holy Spirit has the means to remove the disgusting stones of life.

My first experience with church people happened in my later teen years. By then, I had picked up a few unwholesome habits and actions. Well-meaning church members took it upon themselves to tell me about activities I must quit, places I should avoid, and practices I ought to stop. Their demands only annoyed me and caused greater resistance. Eventually, someone brought me closer to God. The Holy Spirit helped end my destructive conduct.

The history of world missions is filled with both stories of success and failure. Some pioneer missionaries foolishly attempted to westernize other cultures more than tell His story. They tried to reform people to western thinking. Jesus transcends all cultures.

What is your ambition, removing stones or revealing Jesus? The Holy Spirit convicts and convinces transgressors of critical changes needing to be made. He brings to light divine truths. Only He can convince the soul to change.

The Lord does not demand that people change before coming to Him. They come as they are and the Holy Spirit works newness in them. God specializes in removing stones, if you let Him.

Barrier

When the stones of wrongful behavior are removed, what will people see beyond the barrier? Several charges made against church-attending people are well founded. Here are a few commonly heard accusations:

"Too many hypocrites!" People occasionally do hypocritical acts. Believers and non-believers cannot escape this indictment. Everyone could stand to be more real. What better place to be truthful than in a community where behavior is confronted and changes are encouraged?

"Christians don't appear to be better off; they are just as grumpy as everyone else." Some following Jesus fail to enter the joy of salvation; they are more wrapped-up in circumstances than grace. A purified heart is no excuse for a soured disposition.

"Christians are busybodies!" Many could stand to apply the *10/2* principle to their conduct: *Tend to your own business.* Prying uninvited into the lives of others is inappropriate.

"Christians talk about love, but their actions do not show it." Some fail to love everyone, and others fail to love all the time. Only Jesus loves perfectly.

Do your actions create a barrier? Demonstrate overcoming power; reflect His glorious image; be a window of heavenly Sonshine. Seek to be authentic!

ACTION

The words *ministry*, *stone,* and *barrier* are interconnected: they deal with relationships.

Are you actively helping in church? Every believer is gifted for heartfelt and purposeful ministry.

How do you help those still bound by objectionable behavior? Bring them to God! The Holy Spirit effectively removes harmful vices.

How do you act around those needing Jesus? Be a bridge instead of a barrier.

In your life, what will people encounter when the stone has been removed, a resurrected life or just a lot more stink? Accurately represent the resurrected

ACTION

Jesus. Show them the living Lord!

EPILOGUE

PERFECT

The story of Jesus is about a man who lived a perfect life: His thoughts were perfect; His behavior was perfect; His attitude was perfect; His motives were perfect; His desires were perfect; His use of tears was perfect; His use of anger was perfect. All His actions were perfect; He was absolutely sinless.

Did living a perfect life prevent Jesus from having problems and difficulties? Not at all! If you apply yourself with excellence and do everything correctly, will problems stop occurring in your life? Not in this lifetime! Too many relational issues make problem-free living impossible: conflicting personalities; competing ambitions; opposing motives; differing attitudes.

Throughout the book, a recurring statement was

made now needing an additional comment:

If it happened to Jesus, *who is perfect,* it can happen to you—if they did it to Jesus, *who is perfect*, they may do it to you.

No one other than Jesus ever lived a perfect life. If painful and unpleasant circumstances happened to Him, why do you think that by living perfectly you will prevent them?

Jesus truly understands what life can bring. He experienced thoughts and feelings identical to yours, yet He demonstrated love when encountering hate, mercy when suffering abuse, and compassion when experiencing pain.

The good news is that the Lord can channel your actions. The Holy Spirit was sent to strengthen and help you respond like Jesus. Tap into greater grace and power. None of life's challenges can stand up to Him.

ACKNOWLEDGEMENTS

My father, mother, sister, brother, and I grew up on Magnolia Bluff in Seattle, Washington. All of us graduated from Queen Anne High School on Queen Anne hill. Living anywhere but the Pacific Northwest was unimaginable. Church ministry, however, meant experiencing different cultures in the United States, as well as throughout the world.

In every location, close friendships developed with faithful churchmen. They provided important understanding of local customs and encouraged me in my efforts to help people develop a closer walk with Jesus. Without their insight, my actions would have ended in miserable failure. I am indebted to them for augmenting my life and shaping my perspective.

The following men deserve special recognition for influencing and enriching these personal reflections:

Steve Bjorklund, Jack Dorwart, Paul Stoops – Kirkland, Washington

Larry Chapel, Roger Livermore, Richard Plaggemeyer – Livingston, Montana

Carroll Boze, Cliff Gross, Verlin Stetler – Rapid City, South Dakota

Ron Biggar, Pete Boomgarden, Henry Deike – Marshall, Minnesota

Mel Drews, Joe Hammar, Bob Hanson, Clare Wical – Spearfish, South Dakota

Dick Betterly, Russ Carlson, Jerry Clark, Ron DiCianni, Dave Linz, Larry Little, Bob Lowen, Steve Olson, Ron Probst, Mark Shumaker – Mount Prospect, Illinois

Gary Ephraim, Bob Konrath, Daryl Swanson – Palos Heights/ Orland Park, Illinois

Greg Bolt, Joey Dobbs, Paul Handshue, Doug Noyes – Rapid City, South Dakota

and,

Dayton Kingsriter and Steve Tvedt – Trinity Bible College, Ellendale, North Dakota. Both gave essential counsel to a minister responsible for overseeing academicians in an Institution of Higher Education, a different world than the Church. I may have been the recognized leader, but they became my friends.

ABOUT THE AUTHOR

Bob was born and raised in the Pacific Northwest. While serving in the Armed Forces during the Vietnam era, he met his wife, Brenda. They have lived in seven States and raised their four children mostly in the greater Chicago area. They presently reside in southern Missouri.

His career has been as a church overseer, a college administrator, a church denomination leader, a classroom instructor, an athletic coach, and an international emissary.

Bob is an ordained minister, as well as a nationally accredited high school volleyball coach. He is passionate for all generations to enter a life-changing relationship with God and having a fully integrated life through Christ.

He continues to write, teach, and speak in various settings. To view more of his current reflections, his blogs can be found at bob-maddox.blogspot.com. His other ten books are available online.

BOOKS BY THE AUTHOR

SPIRIT Living, *abundantly following Jesus*

GOD, *who are You? Reflections from the names of God in the Bible*

TEN Words, *Reflections from the Ten Commandments*

BLESSING and battles, *Reflections on the Blessing of God and the Battles of Life*

ACTION, *Reflections from the gospel of Mark*

The **CHURCH**, *Reflections from Paul's letter to the Ephesians*

practical **FAITH**, *Reflections from James' letter to the Church*

pure **LOVE**, *Reflections from John's first letter to followers of Jesus*

COMFORT, *Reflections from Paul's second letter to the Corinthians*

really **READY**, *Reflections from the prophetic book of Daniel*

"I Didn't See What Was Coming!", ***LIVING** in Christ*

Available in Hardcover, Paperback, and eBook editions.

www.ingramcontent.com/pod-product-compliance
Lightning Source LLC
Chambersburg PA
CBHW031349040426
42444CB00005B/239